RELEASE YOUR SHACKLES

A CONCISE GUIDE TO LIVING A FREER LIFE

by David Lasocki

PORTLAND, OREGON
INSTANT HARMONY
2018

Published by Instant Harmony, www.instantharmony.net

First printed edition, slightly revised and now corrected, 1 April 2018

Cover design by Laura Serrano Silva
Fonts: Headings, Calibri; text, Book Antiqua

ISBN-13: 978-1986394901
ISBN-10: 1986394905

"Human beings are born free, and everywhere they are in shackles.
Those who believe themselves the master of others are no less enslaved
than they."

Jean-Jacques Rousseau (1762)[1]

"Loyalty to petrified opinions never yet broke a chain or freed
a human soul in this world — and never will."

"It seems to me that a man should secure the 'Well done, faithful servant'
of his own conscience first and foremost, and let all other loyalties go."

Mark Twain (1884)[2]

"Fortunately, some are born with spiritual immune systems that sooner or later give rejection to the illusory worldview grafted upon them from birth through social conditioning. They begin sensing that something is amiss, and start looking for answers. Inner knowledge and anomalous outer experience show them a side of reality others are oblivious to, and so begins their journey of awakening. Each step of the journey is made by following the heart instead of following the crowd and by choosing knowledge over the veils of ignorance."

Henri Bergson[3]

"We can cling to that which is passing, or has already passed, or we can remain accessible to — even surrender to — the creative process, without insisting that we know in advance the ultimate outcome for us, our institutions, or our planet. To accept this challenge is to cherish freedom, to embrace life, and to find meaning."

Stephen Nachmanovitch (1990)[4]

"We shall sooner or later have to give up many of our old habits of thought
and adopt new ones: habits that are better adapted to life in a world that is
living in the presence of the past—and is also living in the presence of the
future and open to continuing creativity."

Rupert Sheldrake (2012)[5]

TABLE OF CONTENTS

UPBEAT

"The aphorism ... is the form of 'eternity.' My ambition is to say in ten
sentences what everyone else says in a book — what everyone else *does not*
say in a book."
(Friedrich Nietzsche, 1889).[6]

"Let us create an explosion on every page, in every paragraph."
(David Shields and Elizabeth Cooperman, 2014)[7]

I started making notes for this book in 2013 and having conversations
about it with my friends. Then it sat on the back burner, simmering in the
heat of my soul and burning a hole in the back of my mind.

At one point in 2016, I became so drowsy for days on end that I
wondered what message Consciousness could possibly be delivering to
me.

A healer friend told me: "You need to write."

"But I *am* writing — a book about music."

"No, not the book in the front of your mind. The one on the back
burner."

I resonated with what she said. So I took out my notes and organized
them into short chapters and sections. I bought a few books by other
people that I had been meaning to read for ages, and I found some other
relevant ones on my bookshelf that I had forgotten about.

What I was reading became so stimulating that my rate of learning
accelerated out of sight, and my life accelerated at an unprecedented rate,
even for me.

Now I understood my mission clearly: to write down all I know in this
moment about being free.

This process led to the e-book version of this book that year.

In 2018, the happy discovery of Create Space has given me an
opportunity to revise the book lightly and have it printed for the first time.

ONE

Literal shackles are rings and chains around our wrists and ankles, ensuring that we stay imprisoned.

The figurative shackles I am dealing with in this book still imprison us, because they create blockages and restrictions — physical, mental, emotional, spiritual, environmental, social, and cultural — in the flow of our life.

We generally don't notice that we have these shackles, because they have become such an intimate part of us.

So the first step in releasing shackles is to recognize and acknowledge that we have them. Then at least those shackles no longer serving us have the potential to be released.

In my experience shackles release when they are good and ready, not a moment sooner. Why would they?

Sometimes they release from only our awareness of their existence; or else the release occurs because our awareness leads to new choices in our lives, or else we discover a new technique that shifts shackles. At other times, the releasing of shackles benefits from a helping hand.

In any case, releasing shackles means, essentially, perceiving life differently.

Part 1 of the book covers some common shackles. Part 2 summarizes background information that I consider essential to my task.

Many methods of releasing shackles have been coming to society in the last ten or twenty years. Part 3 of the book introduces some of the methods that I have been using in my energy-healing work with my clients (and on myself) and have proven effective in my experience.

As the subtitle says, this book is a *concise* guide. Aphorisms and prose poems abound, rather than discussion: concentrated tastes of ideas and methods, to reflect on and to explore further.

For some subjects, a little commentary will be found in the endnotes.

Take a look at the Writings Cited for further reading.

Disclaimer: The material in this book is presented for educational purposes only and is not intended for use in diagnosing or treating any individual.

(Don't) Have a cliché!

A WORD ABOUT THE SUBTITLE

Definitions themselves can be shackles, because they turn our thinking in a particular direction.

But at least they give us a direction, an orientation, from which you and I can start—and start on the same page as we explore our shackles and their release.

According to the *Oxford English Dictionary*,[8] "freer" in the sense of "more free" does not exist in English, only in the sense of someone or something that frees.

But so what?[9] Let's make up new words when they are useful, or new meanings for old words, as people do anyway.

If such monstrosities as "functionality" can be new words, even acknowledged by the distinguished *OED*, why not a new sense of "freer"?

And then my subtitle transforms into a pun: we become more free and we also live the life of people who free ourselves.

PART 1

THE NATURE OF SHACKLES

FREE FORM

In order for human beings to exist in this world, they require form, "The shape, configuration, or structure of something as distinguished from its material."[10]

Our physical body is a form made up of a vast number of nested smaller forms: atoms, molecules, cells, tissues, organs, etc. Each form supports and works in sync with the other forms.

Mentally we also require form, especially in the shape of language, the words and sentences of which enable us to communicate our experience with others.

The words we use about our feelings and emotions give form to them and help us to communicate them to others as well as to ourselves.

All the concepts, ideas, beliefs, practices, and institutions of our cultures also have form.

What do I mean by a cultural practice? Think about driving on the right side of the road. Then think about another element of culture, not so prevalent these days: driving on the left side of the road.

Our environment contains myriad forms, whether natural ones such as trees and plants or human-made ones such buildings and machines.

When the forms we have attracted into our lives are serving us, then we are free. But when any of these forms are no longer serving us in this moment, then we are shackled.

VERSO

Some of the readers of drafts of this book encouraged me to make it more personal, more from my own experience, and less abstract.

Although in a sense the whole book has been filtered through my experience, I knew what they meant. I certainly don't want the book to sound like a textbook, in any way, shape, or form, even free form.

And so, sometimes on the back side of the page — or *verso* as it is called in bibliography — you will find material in which I talk to you directly about my experience of the subject in question.

Here I just wanted to say hello.

FAMILY SHACKLES

Conditioning is the training we receive from our family and society intended to make us think and behave in a certain way.

If such training goes far enough, it may become *conditioning* in the Pavlovian sense of an automatic reaction to something remembered.

In the family we encounter the first people who have ideas about how we should behave, what we should learn, and how fast we should develop. The totality of their ideas creates the family side of our conditioning.

Generally speaking, parents and other relatives believe we should be like them. Of course, they obtained this belief from their own families and cultures, and back and back to the dawn of humanity.

As we ourselves have been controlled, so too we tend to control others, believing it the only way to be.

To reinforce their training, their conditioning, families use systems of reward and punishment:

If you do what I like, if you develop the way I want you to develop and at my tempo, then I will smile at you, praise you, hug you, boast about you to the neighbors, post photos of you on Facebook, feed you candy, and give you bigger presents.

If you don't do what I like, then I will frown at you, raise my voice, criticize you, scold you, guilt-trip you, call you names such as Stubborn or Defiant, tell the neighbors you have "authority issues," lecture you, shout at you, threaten you, stick you in the corner, ground you, shake you, slap you, or worse. Naturally, it's "for your own good."

Yet when anything from our conditioning is not serving our life in this moment, we are shackled.

VERSO

"Conditioning" is one of those fashionable terms — yes, like "functionality" — that I find a little tiresome. I ask myself: "Don't we *already* have a term to describe this phenomenon?" In the case of functionality, we do: function or functions.

In the case of "conditioning," I have to concede that we don't. Teaching? Training? Preparing? Guiding? Habituating? Brain-washing?

With the possible exception of "brain-washing," which is on the right lines but may be too strong, these terms convey different concepts.

So yes, "conditioning" proves to be a useful, even indispensable term.

Just don't confuse it with air conditioning, although the trainers can be windy and the training itself can cause quite a storm....

CULTURAL SHACKLES

Our culture—the society in which we grow up—also has strong ideas about how we should behave, what we should learn, and how fast we should develop. And again, the culture believes that we should be like it.

Its beliefs are taught, propagated, and enforced largely through institutions, such as schools, universities, churches, corporations, the government, the law, and the media.

The beliefs, practices, laws, ideas, and concepts of our culture support and sustain us, but at the same time they control us and they are prone to shackle us.

Cultural institutions often begin with an idea that serves society, then degenerate into perpetuating themselves at all costs.

When culture and its institutions become unquestioned habit, then they have the potential to impose shackles on everyone in that culture.

If we go against our culture, we may well be ridiculed, vilified, attacked, censored, fired, ostracized, exiled, imprisoned, maimed, or killed. Don't think for a moment that the stronger verbs stem from the past, or relate to cultures other than ours. Present-day examples abound. Nevertheless, to be free we must release anything from our culture that is no longer serving us.

VERSO

A reader has taken me to task for seeming to imply that universities (she also said schools) are *necessarily* implements of control, wholly controlling, and nothing but controlling.

So let me go on record as saying: I recognize that the critical thinking taught in universities may sometimes be a means for us to notice our shackles, then release them.

SPIRITUALITY AND RELIGION

I take *spirituality* to be anything connected with matters of the spirit, not the body, mind, or emotions.

I take *religion* to be an institutionalized form of spirituality that has grown up around the spiritual experiences or insights of some individual (e.g., Jesus, Muhammad, or Buddha) in order to disseminate and perpetuate them.

The doctrine that generally follows constitutes a powerful method of control and can easily become a nest of major shackles for the religion's adherents.

In contrast, *mysticism* reflects someone's direct spiritual insight or experience. Most religions have a mystical side, which has often been persecuted.

VERSO

I have deliberately said very little on the subject of religion, about which many people hold powerful beliefs that have enormous influence over their lives.

Please remember that in this book I am trying to draw your attention to anything in your life that may be shackling you. I am not saying that anything is intrinsically "good" or "bad," "beneficial" or "harmful. Well, just wait until I sound off on toxins....

For me the only important test comes in whether something is serving us (in all senses of "us") in this moment.[11]

EDUCATION

The word *education* is derived from the same word in Latin, which "was probably also influenced by association with (ultimately related) classical Latin *educe* ... (with connotations of a person's intrinsic qualities being 'drawn out')."[12]

Most modern education, in contrast, is based on cramming in. We learn what society and the school believe we should learn, at the school's pace, based almost entirely on memorization and repetition, subject to reward and punishment, testing, and grading.[13]

Even when the school offers "electives," we can elect to study them only from the choice the school offers, still on the school's terms.

VERSO

Education has become such a pillar of modern life that we may have difficulty conceiving of any alternative that still serves our children.

So at this point you may wish to skip ahead to the chapter "Unschooling" (p. 79).

I should tip my hand by letting you know that my wife and I have been unschooling our 16-year-old son for the past five years. What I say in the chapter is based on that experience.

BELIEF SYSTEMS AND BS

A *belief system* is "a set of principles, ideas, or convictions"[14] which as a whole make up a religion or a philosophy, whether general or personal.

Our personal belief system determines how we see our lives and how we see the world. It tends to be set in place by our conditioning, confirmed and augmented during our lives by those to whom we accord cognitive authority for second-hand knowledge (see p. 35).

In *every* belief system, certain beliefs, often called "limiting beliefs," create shackles, because they limit our lives in a way that is not serving us in the present.

VERSO

Here I sense that you might appreciate some examples, so let me give you a couple that are common with my clients.

If our parents have continually asked us (rhetorically) "What's wrong with you?" we may develop the belief "There is something wrong with me." Then, whatever we do in life, we harbor the lingering conviction that we will never create what we would like.

Or if we have been bludgeoned by the belief — thankfully now rather old-fashioned — that "Children should be seen and not heard," we may have difficulty speaking up.

LINKS

Shackles may be created by our linking two beliefs in a way that doesn't serve us.

VERSO

Here examples would definitely be useful:

● "If I am loved, I will be punished" — a consequence perhaps of our treatment in childhood, and cutting off our ability to be loved.

● "If I am anxious, I will be loved" — creating anxiety but not attracting love.

● "If I ever get sick, I will become incapacitated" — creating more anxiety about becoming sick.

● "If I make money, I will be humiliated" — of course, limiting our ability to make money.

● "If I make lots of money, then my parents will value me and consider me to be successful" — buying into our parents' (perceived) definitions of value and success.

SELF-X

When I went through lists of words beginning with the prefix "self-" on the Web, I found that more "negative" than "positive" ones exist.

Some of them, shown in the left-hand column below, constitute ways in which we are continuing our conditioning all by ourselves. The opposites of these self-words are shown in the right-hand column.

Self-hate	Self-love
	Self-worth
Self-criticism	Self-acceptance
Self-satisfaction	Self-approval
Self-sabotage	Self-support
Self-abandonment	
Self-abuse	
Self-abasement	
Self-aggrandizement	
Self-annihilation	
Self-castigation	
Self-condemnation	
Self-contempt	
Self-deprecation	
Self-destruction	Self-belief
Self-mortification	
Self-sacrifice	
Self-reproach	Self-forgiveness
Self-reproof	Self-determination
Self-deception	Self-honesty
Self-flattery	
Self-doubt	Self-confidence
Self-denial	Self-nurture

VERSO

Other self-words deliver a mixed message: they could be more ways in which we are beating ourselves up; or they demonstrate how others may label us when we start to release our conditioning and take care of ourselves.

Self-absorbed
Self-centered
Self-serving
Self-indulgent
Self-involved
Self-seeking
Selfish
Self-righteous

In either case, if we turn this last set of words into their opposites, we come up with virtues that result from releasing self-shackles.

Self-aware
Self-reliant
Self-assured
Self-preserving
Self-starting
Self-sufficient
Selfless

FOOD FOR LIFE

For most of its existence, humanity has had to eat animals and plants living in its environment, or products derived from them.

Nowadays, because of the prevalence of trade at long distances, food grown in one climate commonly makes its way to people living in other climates.

Moreover, an enormous food industry has grown up to process food and, in the process, add chemicals to sweeten, color, flavor, and preserve the food.

The food for most of us these days is based on some mixture of:
- what we ate as children,
- what we have learned generally from our culture, including imports from other cultures,
- what we find in the stores or at the market,
- what is advertised,
- the latest fashions, such as paleo, raw, and vegan.

In other words, we largely eat what other people have influenced us to eat.

Sometimes the influence of science and the media can be misleading, as in the faulty research and blind reporting about saturated fats.[15] Then what everybody in society "knows" serves no one.

When our food does not serve who we are in this moment, then we are shackled. Even when something served us last week, is it still serving us today? Let's check.

VERSO

Food is close to people's minds and hearts and souls as well as their bodies. For this reason, I have found discussing it with people a challenging path to tread.

To let me take a deep breath and tell you (concisely) about my own experience of food and shackles.

I grew up in England, consuming vast quantities of sugared tea. By my mid-teens I was having trouble concentrating and memorizing my school work. By the time I reached university I could barely function, physically or mentally, and I graduated by the skin of my teeth.

On coming to the United States to attend graduate school, I discovered Macrobiotics, "Big Life," which promised health through locally grown natural foods in season. Through reading the works of its founder, George Ohsawa (1893–1966), and his leading former student Michio Kushi (1926–2014), I became convinced that food was the secret to health, perhaps even the only secret.[16] The basis of macrobiotics was the Taoist principle of the balance of yin and yang forces in the universe, which became a great influence on my thinking.

I took the plunge and became "macrobiotic." Soon I was eating a Japanese-inspired vegan diet of whole grains, miso soup, sautéed vegetables, aduki beans and tofu, kukicha tea (until I realized it contained caffeine), and such delightful natural deserts as apple strudel with whole wheat puff pastry. I had always been thin, but now I became emaciated, much to my teachers' alarm. A "true believer," I didn't share their alarm, but pressed on regardless. It was at least another twenty years before I regained the lost weight (after adding almond butter to my breakfast). But physically and mentally I did recover, and in time I was able to complete my studies through the doctoral level.

Over the last 45 years, I have added dairy, eggs, chicken, and fish to what I eat, and sometimes subtracted them again, but I have never returned to sugar, caffeine, alcohol, or red meat. At the moment, I find that no form of meat serves me.

People I encounter are usually incredulous that I could avoid sugar for so long. But honestly, if I ever get something containing sugar in my mouth, the intensity and quality of the sweetness literally hurt my mouth, so I couldn't possibly eat that food.

I came to realize in time that a fanatical adherence to any system of eating can be a huge shackle. Although I couldn't declare that I have moved completely beyond "true believer," I do check with myself at every meal and snack about what my body would like—what food would serve me—in that moment.

In working with clients, I have observed that people can use sugar, chocolate, alcohol, and smoking as ways to suppress uncomfortable emotions. If clients make jokes about certain foods or drinks they are consuming, then it's even more likely that emotional suppression is occurring. Anything that we suppress creates a shackle.

(This page has been left intentionally blank. Or perhaps you could consider it as a representation of Consciousness.)

TOXINS

Toxins — poisonous substances — have become so prevalent in modern life that they beggar the imagination.

Toxins are commonly found in water, food and drink, household products, personal-care products, cosmetics, perfumes, chemtrails, vaccinations, furnishings, and building materials, not to mention amalgam fillings. All of them have the potential to shackle us bigtime.

One of our biggest shackles may be incredulity that the environment could be so poisoned.

Are all corporations benevolent? Are the Food and Drug Administration, Federal Trade Commission, and Department of Agriculture protecting us adequately?

For example, GMOs have not been tested for their long-term effects. Can you trust them?[17]

Can we really put mercury, a cumulative toxin, in our mouths and leave it there for decades without suffering harm?[18]

Pesticide residues such as glyphosate abound on our food, if it's not organic, and even organic food is becoming contaminated from the environment. What effect does eating this food have on us?

How about drinking water to which "safe" quantities of hazardous waste, a known neurotoxin, are added in the interest of dental health?[19]

Is WiFi safe? Radiation from computers and cell phones?

VERSO

As you will have gathered, I feel strongly about the way our environment is being poisoned.

A reader objected: "Any chemical, natural or synthesized, is toxic to humans at a high enough concentration/dosage. These are risks that we take on as humans living in a modern society, and risks can only be estimated, whether by corporations (true that they might be biased), the government, or scientists."

Agreed, but my point is that we are unwittingly being used as guinea pigs because we are relying on others, who may not have our best interests at heart, to estimate the risks for us.

We must inform ourselves of the risks and take care of ourselves.

More than twenty years ago, I became aware of some of the toxins in my environment and began to take action. I had the mercury fillings in my teeth replaced. I was already eating organic food as much as possible, and fortunately that has become more widely available these days as consumer demand has grown. I switched to the simplest natural personal-care products. My family and I started to filter our drinking and shower water. And so on. Nowadays I always use headphones with my cell phone and never leave it in my pocket for long.

We can all take such simple precautions.

IT'S NOT MUTUAL

- Blaming
- Name-calling
- Complaining
- Criticizing without being invited[20]
- Insisting that we have the right answer
- Lecturing other people
- Even offering unsolicited advice

All these behaviors force our opinions and perspective on others in an attempt to control them, consciously or not.

Such behavior puts a damper on the free flow of feedback in relationships, contributing to *our own* shackles.

IN THE SHADOW?

In Jungian psychology, the "shadow" is seen as the aspects of our personality of which we are not fully conscious.[21]

Anything about ourselves that we are not cognizant of can be a shackle.

In common parlance, the term "shadow" refers to the "negative" side of our thoughts, desires, and behavior that we would rather not acknowledge.

Inasmuch as we are not acknowledging this side, it can be a shackle.

DRUGGED OUT

Sign seen in a drugstore:
"Just say no to drugs."

We commonly use the word *drug* in three main senses:

(1) "a natural or synthetic substance used in the prevention or treatment of disease";

(2) "a substance with intoxicating, stimulant, or narcotic effects used for cultural, recreational, or other non-medicinal purposes."[22]

(3), which also reflects on the first two: "something, and often an illegal substance, that causes addiction, habituation, or a marked change in consciousness."[23]

The humor in the quotation at the head of this section stems, of course, from the dissonance between senses (1) and (3).

Drug can also be used in the figurative sense of: (4) "Something regarded as having properties similar to those of a drug, especially (in later use) in being addictive"[24] — for example, sex, money, TV, the Internet, smart phones, applause, or adulation.

Addictive substances and phenomena shackle us by impeding our free choice.

We might not acknowledge the most common recreational drugs in our society: caffeine,[25] alcohol, and nicotine (the active ingredient in tobacco). They far exceed the use of marijuana, legal or otherwise, and hard drugs.

According to the CDC (Centers for Disease Control and Prevention), the most lethal drugs in our society are tobacco, alcohol, and opoid-based prescription painkillers.[26]

All medicinal drugs are said to have "side-effects," listed in small print. In truth, "side-effects" are just effects, unwanted for medical purposes but present nonetheless.

When a substance is taken out of its natural context and highly concentrated — for example, sugar out of sugar cane or sugar beets — it takes on some of the qualities of a drug.[27] I'm talking about sucrose, not the family of sugars, although high-fructose corn syrup is on the rise, sometimes in disguise. Recent scientific evidence suggests that sugar is eight times as addictive as cocaine.[28] Surprised?

VERSO

Yes, I know I have come back to sugar. But my overall purpose in this chapter is to mention addiction, conscious or inadvertent, and to begin our exploration of alternatives to the medicines that address only the chemical side of human beings.

Lots more about this in parts 2 and 3, so let's move on.

PART 2

ESSENTIAL BACKGROUND

"OBJECTIVE" AND "SUBJECTIVE"

Two completely different approaches to gaining knowledge are available to us. For the sake of simplicity, I am calling these approaches "objective" and "subjective."

Objective

The objective approach is most readily seen in science, which seeks theories of exterior experience that can be tested and verified. As Edward O. Wilson wrote, "Science, to put its warrant as concisely as possible, is the organized, systematic enterprise that gathers knowledge about the world and condenses the knowledge into testable laws and principles."[29]

Science relies on a community of scientists to gain expertise, usually within a particular subfield of science, to conduct experiments, and to make sense of their findings by coming up with theories. Scientists report their findings and present their theories to the community, which then tests the reproducibility of the findings. When the community has some degree of consensus that the findings are reproducible and the theories always explain the findings, the theories are considered to have been verified.

The system of peer review in the community provides essential anonymous feedback about the quality of the research and the theories. Yet peer review tests only the methods and reasoning of submitted papers, not the data, which is left to be ironed out by subsequent experiments by others. Nevertheless, if the system is working well, "the scientific method transcends the flaws of individual scientists."[30]

Evidence is now accumulating, however, at least in biomedicine and experimental psychology, that the claims of most scientific papers cannot be replicated.[31] Evidence is also accumulating about the "file drawer effect": the tendency for scientists to publish only results that support their research agendas.[32]

Moreover, the system may perpetuate existing theories at the expense of new ones. Belief systems and politics die hard.

Some people consider the scientific approach to be the only valid approach, and one that produces certain knowledge. For example, the physicist Robert Park states that "Science is the only way we have of separating the truth from ideology, or fraud, or mere foolishness."[33]

Park labels anything that doesn't follow the scientific method "voodoo science," classified into "pathological science" (in which scientists fool themselves into believing they have made a great discovery), "junk science" or "fraudulent science" (in which scientists or others deliberately fool people into believing they have created something that disobeys the laws of science), and "pseudoscience" (beliefs and claims for which there is no evidence).[34]

Yet science tends to neglect our interior experience. What is the "truth" of that?

Anything based on interior experience may be labeled "pseudoscience," not to mention new theories that challenge the belief systems of scientists. Witness the treatment of Rupert Sheldrake, whose first book was labeled "the best candidate for burning there has been for many years," "magic instead of science," and even "heresy" by a leading science editor.[35] More on Sheldrake soon (p. 41).

Above all, we must bear in mind that all scientific theories will eventually be considered incorrect or, at least, incomplete.

Subjective
Of course, everyone has interior experience. We can all agree that we hear, see, smell, taste, and touch; we think; and we feel emotion and sensation.

Some people also acknowledge mystical experience: an interior connection with Consciousness.

A mystical approach to gaining knowledge has been practiced in the spiritual traditions for thousands of years. Individuals test their interior experience in the laboratory of their own meditation practice. Then they compare notes about this interior experience with their teachers, and ultimately with a community of others who are following similar practices.

Eventually, a body of knowledge, a map, grows based on inner, subjective experience verified by a community.[36]

The two approaches, both valid in their own way, are complementary.

COGNITIVE AUTHORITY

Let us call knowledge that has been gained through our own experience, whether by objective or subjective means, "first-hand knowledge."

Most of our knowledge, however, actually comes from other people, or what Patrick Wilson called "second-hand knowledge."[37]

We have tested little of that knowledge ourselves. Nor would it be realistic to test more than the tiniest fraction of the world's knowledge, even in a field we know well.

To whom are we led for second-hand knowledge? "... those whom we think know something we do not know."[38] But how do we decide who knows about what? "That is a question about *cognitive authority*.... Some people know what they are talking about, others do not. Those who do are my cognitive authorities."[39] So we decide, consciously or unconsciously, which people seem to know what they are talking about.

"... cognitive authority is a matter of degree: one can have a little of it or a lot." And cognitive authority is restricted to a sphere of knowledge. We may trust people in one sphere but not in others.

A cognitive authority, a person to whom we have given cognitive authority, is different from an expert, who might have expertise but not be recognized by us (or anyone else).[40]

And, I should add, we might give cognitive authority to people who are not experts but give the appearance of being experts or are simply confident about what they are saying— cocktail-party orators. As a teacher of mine sagely remarked, "Confidence is not the same as knowledge."

Taken to its extreme, cognitive authority can become "charismatic authority." "The prophet, the hero, the saint may attract a complete personal devotion that carries with it a readiness to let the individual define his own sphere of cognitive authority. In less extreme cases, we may be so impressed by a person, so attracted or mesmerized by him, that we are prepared to believe whatever he says."[41] Let us add politicians and great scientists to Wilson's list: witness the devotion to Einstein in quotations being thrown around the Web.

Cognitive authority rests not only in people, but also in books, publishers, websites, organizations, institutions, and disciplines. Science, for example, has cognitive authority for most people today, and religion still does for many.

Cognitive authority differs from administrative authority, which "involves a recognized right to command others, within certain prescribed limits." Someone with cognitive authority cannot tell people what to think, but rather "is a kind of influence."

INTERNETTED

The Internet (World Wide Web) is commonly said to have transformed research. "You can find everything you need online now, and so easily."

To my mind, the Internet presents the same pitfalls as pre-online research and a good many more.

To be sure, the Internet places vast amounts of data at our disposal. But before we can call this data information, not to mention "second-hand knowledge," we must apply our critical faculties.

Yes, I *am* implying the question: How much of the data on the Internet is reliable— accurate, up-to-date, unbiased, thorough, and written by people to whom we would accord cognitive authority? And do the more reliable data come to the fore readily in searches?

To carry out the most effective and efficient research requires developing what librarians call *information literacy*, in parallel with literacy in language, "clearly the new basic skill set of the 21st century."[42] It includes, among other things, determining all possible sources, selecting the most reliable, locating them, and extracting relevant information.

If we are not information-literate, we run the risk of shackling ourselves with information that doesn't serve us.[43]

QUANTUM LEAPING

Quantum theory (quantum mechanics, quantum physics), which began to be developed over a century ago, holds sway in science, because all experiments designed to test its predictions have been unable to show that any part of the theory is incorrect.[44]

Quantum theory caused such a revolution that the world — even the community of quantum physicists — has barely begun to catch up with its implications. One of its founders, Niels Bohr, wrote: "Anyone not shocked by quantum mechanics has not understood it."[45]

Most people today are stuck in the worldview of Newtonian science, dating from the seventeenth century. Yes, believe it or not, most people are living from a belief system more than four hundred years behind science. Serious shackles here!

In the Newtonian view, the position and velocity of objects are predictable ("determinism"); nature is a kind of machine, which exists independent of its observation ("realism"); every object is separate from the rest of the universe, interacting only through physical forces ("separability"); and complex systems are the sum of their parts ("reduction").

Three fundamental aspects of quantum theory have shattered the Newtonian worldview:

First, no "realism." The universe exists in a state that quantum theory calls "superposition," in which an object is in more than one place at the same time. Mathematically, the state can be represented by a wave function. What enables the object to come into physical reality, to be in only one place, is *conscious observation.*

Mathematically, the wave function changing to an observed single reality is known as the "collapse" of the wave function, or more commonly nowadays, its "decoherence."

According to this theory, consciousness brings the physical universe into being.

Such a notion is still controversial with quantum physicists, who have come up with a variety of approaches to whether consciousness has to be brought into a theory about physical reality and, if so, how consciousness could interact with that reality.

Second, no "separability" or "reduction." "... any two objects that have ever interacted are forever entangled. The behavior of one instantaneously influences the other. An entanglement exists even if the interaction is through each of the objects having interacted with a third object. In principle, our world has a universal connectedness."[46]

Physically, everything in the universe is connected. Note that everything is connected not by energy or by awareness, which would take time to travel: it is connected instantaneously.

Third, no "determinism." As Heisenberg's Uncertainly Principle established, the more accurately we measure an object's position, the more uncertain we will be about its speed (and vice versa).

ZPF

Another group of theories in modern physics, about the Zero Point Field, may not have received as much experimental confirmation as quantum theory, but they do suggest answers to some of the mysteries of that theory.[47]

At absolute zero, the lower limit of the thermodynamic temperature scale (–273.15 degrees C or –459.67 degrees F), exists "the lowest possible state of energy, where all matter has been removed and nothing is supposedly left to make any motion."[48] But "lowest possible state" doesn't imply that no energy exists.

Heisenberg's Uncertainty Principle also means "that we cannot know both the energy and the lifetime of a particle, so a subatomic event occurring within a tiny time frame involves an uncertain amount of energy..... all elementary particles interact with each other by exchanging energy through other quantum particles, which are believed to appear out of nowhere, combining and annihilating each other in less than an instant ... causing random fluctuations of energy without any apparent cause. The fleeting particles generated during this brief moment are known as 'virtual particles.' They differ from real particles because they only exist during that exchange — the time of uncertainty allowed by the Uncertainty Principle.... This subatomic tango, however brief, when added across the universe, gives rise to enormous energy, more than is contained in all the matter in all the world."[49] "More" proves to be an enormous understatement: "It has been calculated that the total energy of the Zero Point Field exceeds all energy in matter by a factor of 10^{40}, or 1 followed by 40 zeros."[50]

As put forward in theories by Hal Puthoff, subatomic particles are in constant dynamic exchange with the Zero Point Field, literally making waves. "... fluctuations of the Zero Point Field waves drive the motion of subatomic particles and ... all the motion of all the particles of the universe in turn generates the Zero Point Field, a sort of self-generating feedback loop across the cosmos."[51]

Because waves encode and carry information (through constructive and destructive interference), "the subatomic waves of The [Zero Point] Field are constantly imprinting a record of the shape of everything. As the harbinger [announcer] and imprinter of all wavelengths and all frequencies, the Zero Point Field is a kind of shadow of the universe for all time, a mirror image and record of everything that ever was."[52]

The Zero Point Field provides alternative explanations to quantum theory of wave–particle duality and nonlocality. "Quantum physics most famously claims that a particle can also simultaneously be a wave unless observed and then measured, when all its tentative possibilities collapse into a set entity. With Hal's theory, a particle is always a particle, but its state just seems indeterminate because it is constantly interacting with this background energy field," the Zero Point Field.[53] "... what if it were zero-point fluctuation that was the underlying mechanism acting on quantum entities and causing one entity to affect the other? If that were true, it mean[s] every part of the universe could be in touch with every other part instantaneously."[54]

KRISHNA'S TAPESTRY AND THE QUESTION OF CONSCIOUSNESS

The question of consciousness has long been addressed in the spiritual traditions—for example, by Advaita Vedanta in India. A development of its philosophy due to one of my teachers, Krishna Gauci, provides the useful framework I will discuss here.[55]

Consciousness has been referred to by many other names, such as God, Spirit, Source, the Divine, the Self, the Ground of Being, Brahman, Buddha Nature, Christ Consciousness, Spacious Awareness, and Unconditioned Awareness.

Consciousness resists definition, because it has no attributes in the normal sense, and cannot be experienced or observed. I have my own sense of it as Presence, Inspiration, Completeness, and Sufficiency.

In the realm of Consciousness, the term *shackles* is meaningless. There we are "always already free."[56]

Out of Consciousness, a field of Radiant Energy "comes into manifestation and is the substance of all that is experienced."[57]

Radiant Energy is Krishna's deliberately neutral term for what has been referred to by many other names. In Hindu Tantra (Trika), it is known as Vimarsa (Reflection), Spanda (Vibration), Mahashakti (Supreme Energy), or the Great Goddess.

This field of Radiant Energy can be experienced, felt, in mystical experience as Bliss, Presence, or Shakti.

In mystical experience, we also realize that we and the field are One. We recognize the field as ourselves. No separation.

The field of Radiant Energy creates the experience of physical reality for our senses.

And within this sensed experience, the observer (us) and the observed (physical reality) arise simultaneously and interdependently.

CORRELATIONS

Let us note the apparent correlations between the objective exterior experience of science and the subjective interior experience of spirituality:
- between the Zero Point Field (science) and the field of Radiant Energy (spirituality);
- between the universal connectedness (no separability) of science and the universal connectedness (no separation) of spirituality;
- between the observer creating reality (science) and the observer and the observed arising simultaneously and interdependently (spirituality).

Nevertheless, science and spirituality, the "objective" and the "subjective," are different practices, valuable in their own ways, that cannot be equated with one another and do not "verify" one another.

MORPH(OGEN)IC FIELDS

Recall that form may be defined as "The shape, configuration, or structure of something as distinguished from its material."[58] Everything in this universe has form, whether the "things" are physical, mental, emotional, spiritual, environmental, social, or cultural.

So how is that form created and maintained? Why, for example, don't the atoms and molecules that make up physical things just fly off into space? This is a vital subject that science has hardly addressed.

One living scientist, Rupert Sheldrake, has proposed a hypothesis about the subject that I find persuasive, as well as valuable in releasing shackles.[59] Because this hypothesis has challenged the culture of science, which is ostensibly based on proposing and testing hypotheses, he has been ridiculed, vilified, physically attacked, censored, ostracized, and (self-) exiled. Fortunately, he remains with us, teaching, writing, calmly answering his critics, and designing experiments to test his hypotheses without the benefit of scientific funding.

The main reason for the hostility to Sheldrake is that modern science is generally based on mechanistic theories, which treat the universe and everything in it as machines. He explains that "In biology, the mechanistic theory states that living organisms are nothing but inanimate machines or mechanical systems; all the phenomena of life can in principle be understood in terms of mechanical models and can ultimately be explained in terms of physics and chemistry."[60]

Sheldrake, in contrast, has proposed hypotheses based on organicism, "A form of holism according to which the world consists of organisms ... at all levels of complexity. Organisms are wholes made up of parts, which are themselves organisms, and so on; they are organized in nested hierarchies. The parts of organisms can be understood only in relation to their activities and functions in the ongoing whole. Organisms in this sense include atoms, molecules, crystals, cells, tissues, organs, plants and animals, societies, cultures, ecosystems, planets, planetary systems, and galaxies. In this spirit, the entire cosmos can be regarded as an organism rather than as a machine."[61]

Part of Sheldrake's answer to my questions about form is that each unit of form — an atom, a molecule, a crystal, a cell, a plant, an animal, a human being, a planet, a galaxy — has a *field* around and within it, a region of influence, that organizes its structure and its patterns of activity. A field may seem a little vague compared with the concreteness of physical form, but I am sure you are already familiar with electromagnetic fields. Did you ever do an experiment in physics where you put a bar magnet underneath a sheet of paper and sprinkle some iron filings on top of the paper? The iron filings spread themselves out to show the magnetic field around the magnet.

The adjective *morphic* is derived from the Ancient Greek word *morph*, meaning "Of or relating to form or shape."[62] According to Sheldrake, the term *morphogenetic field* was first proposed in the 1920s to describe biological fields "that play a causal role in morphogenesis" (the coming into being of form).[63] This term "is now widely used by developmental biologists, but the nature of morphogenetic fields remains obscure" (to those scientists).

Sheldrake has been responsible for clarifying the concept of morphogenetic field, bringing it into the quantum science era, and exploring its implications at length. A more general term, *morphic field*, may now be defined as "A field within and around a morphic unit that organizes its characteristic structure and pattern of activity. Morphic fields underlie the form and behavior of holons, or morphic units, at all levels of complexity."[64] The term "includes morphogenetic, behavioral, social, cultural, and mental fields."

How do these fields work? Sheldrake proposes that morphic fields are shaped and stabilized by the influence of previous *similar* morphic units, which were under the influence of fields of the same kind. Such influence passes through space and time, and doesn't seem to fall off with either space or time. He calls this influence *morphic resonance*.[65] In general usage, the word *resonance* means a "corresponding or sympathetic response."[66]

Your body has a morphic field, and all its parts have a large number of nested morphic fields. Your torso contains your liver, which is made up of cells, which are made up of molecules, etc. Each of these morphic units is organized by morphic fields. The overarching field of your body has morphic resonance in general with the morphic fields of all previous humans. Morphic fields never go away, and they become stronger the more they shape form. The general morphic fields of all previous humans are now very strong, because they have been shaping form for thousands of years.

Your body also has morphic resonance in particular with all of the previous instances of the morphic field of your body, going back to your birth, and maybe earlier. All of the instances of your body's morphic field constitute a kind of cumulative memory of your body. Your body, through the morphic resonance of the instances of its morphic field, has the habit of showing up more or less the same way in every moment. And the more it practices morphic resonance, the more it tends to show up in the same way.

Sheldrake's main contribution to science is what he calls the "hypothesis of formative causation."[67] This is a grand way of saying what I have already mentioned: that morphic units at all levels of complexity are organized by morphic fields, which are influenced and stabilized by morphic resonance from all previous similar morphic units.

Now, you may ask, why don't morphic units show up in *exactly* the same way each time? If my body has self-morphic resonance with my body five minutes ago, and my body in five minutes will have self-morphic resonance with my body now, why doesn't my body stay the same? The answer is that in this quantum universe, nothing is completely predictable.[68] Neither is anything completely determinate. This is immediately obvious when we think of the leaves on a tree: they are all similar to one another, and similar to leaves on other trees of the same species, but no two leaves are identical. Even if the leaves are genetically identical and grow on the same tree in virtually the same conditions, no two leaves are identical. Even if the species has been around for a thousand years and its morphic resonance has had a chance to become very strong, no two leaves are identical.

So the probabilistic and indeterminate nature of morphic fields allows for variations on a theme: a leaf, a human being. And looking at it another way, this nature allows for creative ways of dealing with circumstances. If the circumstances change, the morphic field has room to change. Even new morphic fields can come into existence, by a mysterious creative leap or synthesis. More complex fields can evolve from simpler ones, or simpler fields can originate within more complex fields.

The tendency for morphic fields to show up more or less the same each time can be viewed as a kind of habit. Without habit, nothing could exist in form. So habit is useful for creating form. At the same time, when the circumstances change, habit can get in the way, by not allowing the morphic fields to change appropriately in response. And then, to return to the theme of the present book, we become shackled.

You may have understood from what I have been saying that morphic fields are holders of memory. The mechanistic theory posits that memory depends on some material traces in the nervous system. According to Sheldrake's hypothesis of formative causation, memory is due to morphic resonance with a vast number of morphic fields.

Here's a phenomenon that struck me forcibly when I was reading Sheldrake's books. A human embryo contains only one kind of cell. But eventually these initially identical cells become part of very different parts of the body: muscles, skin, liver, brain, etc. How do the initial cells know how to differentiate themselves like this? Is it because of a gene that somehow mysteriously possesses a memory to carry out this procedure?[69] Or is the gene just a chemical, after all, and some other force is also at work in the body? According to Sheldrake, the embryo has morphic resonance with the morphic fields of past human beings.

Morphic fields never seem to go away, but are always available, even when new morphic fields have been created. For example, if domesticated pigs are released into the wild, they turn into feral pigs, and these feral pigs become more bristly, they tend to redevelop their tusks, and the stripes of young wild pigs reappear in their offspring.[70] Sheldrake's interpretation is that the pigs in wild circumstances now have resonance with the morphic fields of wild pigs instead of domesticated pigs.

In the energy-medicine systems I learned, it is taken for granted that Sheldrake's hypothesis of morphic fields is true,[71] although they are called *matrixes* instead, and the term has become installed in popular culture through the movie *The Matrix*. Cultural and social morphic fields are often called *memes*.[72]

(Another blank page.)

ENERGY IS ETERNAL DELIGHT

The term "energy" has proven essential to physics, although as Richard Feynman confessed in a famous lecture, "It is important to realize that in physics today, we have no knowledge of what energy is."[73]

Feynman defines energy in relation to the physical law of the conservation of energy, which states that "there is a certain quantity, which we call energy, that does not change in the manifold changes which nature undergoes. That is a most abstract idea, because it is a mathematical principle; it says that there is a numerical quantity which does not change when something happens. It is not a description of a mechanism, or anything concrete; it is just a strange fact that we can calculate some number and when we finish watching nature go through her tricks and calculate the number again, it is the same."

As normally stated, not in Feynman's disarming insight, the total energy of an isolated system remains constant (conserved) over time; energy can neither be created nor destroyed, but may transform from one form to another.

Feynman adds: " ... the energy has a large number of different forms, and there is a [mathematical] formula for each one. These are: gravitational energy, kinetic energy, heat energy, elastic energy, electrical energy, chemical energy, radiant energy, nuclear energy, mass energy." He also acknowledges potential energy ("energy which has to do with location relative to something else"), which can take the form of electrical potential energy, gravitational potential energy, etc.

In everyday life, *energy* also refers to enthusiasm, effort, vigor, the ability to be active, or even the display of power.

In this book, especially in the term *energy healing*, I use *energy* as a handy synonym for what the Chinese call *qi* or *ch'i* (Japanese, *ki*; Korean, *gi*; Hindi, *prana*), which approximates to "life force."

Is *qi* different from the other forms of energy that have been recognized by physicists so far? From what I have read, that is an open question.[74] James Oschman, who summarizes recent scientific research on the human body, suggests that "healing energy" has a thermal (heat) component and a biomagnetic component (magnetic fields that scan through a variety of frequencies in the extremely low frequency, or ELF, range).[75] But that may not be the whole story.

Recent research has shown that the acupuncture meridians—in Chinese "rivers of *qi*" — are located on the connective tissue and fascia, and also seem to correspond to a newly discovered circulatory system called the primo vascular system (PVS).[76]

From the viewpoint of subjective experience, *qi* can be felt as movement within the body, received by the body, and projected by the body. Just ask practitioners of acupuncture, energy healing, or any Eastern martial art such as Qi Gong.

VERSO

"Energy is eternal delight." I couldn't resist using as a heading this well-known saying from William Blake's *The Marriage of Heaven and Hell* (1793).[77]
But did you know the context for the saying?

"Without Contraries is no progression. Attraction and Repulsion, Reason and Energy, Love and Hate, are necessary to Human existence. From these contraries spring what the religious call Good & Evil. Good is the passive that obeys Reason. Evil is the active springing from Energy. Good is Heaven. Evil is Hell. The voice of the Devil: All Bibles or sacred codes have been the causes of the following Errors: 1. That Man has two real existing principles, Viz.: a Body & a Soul. 2. That Energy, call'd Evil, is alone from the Body, & that Reason, call'd Good, is alone from the Soul. 3. That God will torment Man in Eternity for following his Energies. But the following Contraries to these are True: 1. Man has no Body distinct from his Soul; for that call'd Body is a portion of Soul discern'd by the five Senses, the chief inlets of Soul in this age. 2. Energy is the only life and is from the Body, and Reason is the bound or outward circumference of Energy. 3. Energy is Eternal Delight."

In other words, Blake is not talking about energy in any of the present-day senses, but rather, the creative principle as opposed to the rational principle, both of which he considers necessary to life. I will have more to say about these two principles in Part 3.

ENERGY HEALING

"Healing" means "restoring wholeness."

The terms "energy healing" or "energy medicine" refer to unblocking or strengthening the body's *qi* and psyche by a multitude of energy techniques or, to use a fashionable word, "modalities," so that we become whole again.

Such modalities belong to a wider sphere known as complementary and alternative medicine (CAD).

One such modality, BodyTalk, is founded on the insight that we have an innate ability to heal ourselves — an ability that can be addressed by the innate ability of a skilled energy practitioner.

Each modality possesses a strong morphic field (matrix) of its own that supports its techniques and practitioners, becoming stronger with every class and every session.

Practitioners don't diagnose, cure, or fix, but facilitate the healing process.

Healing can take place in person or at a distance.

Energy healing does not necessarily mean beaming *qi* at people and allowing it to take its course, although some of the simpler modalities do just that.

The most powerful modalities benefit from a detailed knowledge of anatomy and physiology, Traditional Chinese Medicine, belief systems, cultural practices, and matrixes. These modalities work on every level of someone's energy — physical, mental, emotional, spiritual, environmental, and cultural — as well as on the morphic fields.

James Oschman cites recent scientific studies that demonstrate the efficacy of energy healing and he suggests mechanisms by which it could work.[78] These mechanisms illustrate scientific discoveries of the last few decades showing that the body works in a completely different way than twentieth-century medical textbooks describe.[79]

I also suggest that the intention of the practitioner (coupled with the practitioner's knowledge of what to intend) "collapses the wave function," in quantum theory terms.

Energy healing can also be verified subjectively, through the shared experience of the healer and the person healed. Thousands of people who have experienced such techniques for themselves can testify that they work.

Healing at a distance can exist because everything in the universe is instantaneously connected, so distance poses no limitation to intention.

VERSO

I have been a practicing energy healer of various modalities for about twenty years now, cycling through vibrational essences, Reiki, Magnified Healing, LaHoChi, BodyTalk, Yuen Mastery, and Matrix Energetics. At the moment, I use a mixture of these modalities, along with new techniques that come to me through my practice almost every week.

So when I tell you that energy healing can be a powerful way to release shackles, it comes from my experience with my clients and with myself.

Would energy healing work for you? Yes, if you are open to its effects. I have experienced that, because our experience is largely a product of our belief systems, people can block the effects.

INTUITION

Intuition is one of the most important ways in which we can gain "first-hand knowledge."

Intuition is usually defined as "The immediate apprehension of an object by the mind without the intervention of any reasoning process," " Immediate apprehension by sense," or "In a more general sense: Direct or immediate insight."[80] Instances of intuition are of course called *intuitions.*[81]

Rollin McCraty distinguishes three different types of intuition, of which the one just defined is the first, called *implicit knowledge.*[82] It draws on the ability of the (right) brain "to rapidly and unconsciously recognize important cues" that we are seeing or hearing "and match them to familiar ones."[83] Such knowledge does also seem to be responsible for the "aha!" or "Eureka" kind of insight.[84]

Second, *nonlocal intuition,* which accounts for premonitions about a person or event.[85] A HeartMath experiment showed that participants' hearts and then brains could respond to an emotionally charged photograph about five seconds before the photograph was randomly selected by a computer.

Where do intuitions of the first two types come from? Apparently from our subconscious, which has a direct connection with Radiant Energy, beyond space and time as well as the sense of self.

Intuitions can come in the form of thoughts, emotions, feelings, sensations, images, smells, clues, and hunches.

Third, *energetic sensitivity,* or "the ability of our body and nervous system to detect electromagnetic and other types of energetic signals in the environment." The HeartMath Institute performed scientific experiments demonstrating that "a subtle yet influential electromagnetic or 'energetic' communication system operates just below our conscious awareness [that] energetically connects us to others and helps explain how we can feel or sense another person's presence or their emotional state."[86]

VERSO

In my experience, intuition (awareness) develops gradually, as we learn to pay attention to it, to trust it, and — after many regrets about not following it — to take action based on it. We are more inclined to trust it, the more that following it produces what we deem to be a beneficial outcome, and I don't mean necessarily a material one.

I find that intuition, in the first sense of implicit knowledge, actually works best when it is based on a body of knowledge we have acquired on a particular subject. This intuition has to work on *something*.

My own experience of intuition extends to "rating" decisions or options on a scale of one to ten, for the highest good of all concerned.

If I receive no answer, or if a have a series of options that all receive six out of ten, I trust that the answer will come later, or else I need to collect more information beforehand.

Intuition tends to have a bad reputation, as if it beggars logic. But follow the progression of subjective experience and see where it leads.

"I FEEL, THEREFORE I AM";
OR, PUTTING DE HEART BEFORE DESCARTES

"Je pense, donc je suis."
(I think, therefore I am.)
René Descartes (1637)[87]

In conventional education, we receive a great deal of instruction that requires us to use our minds. Although thinking does indeed make up a vital part of being human, little or no instruction is given in feelings or intuition.

But feelings also make up a vital part of being human, providing a rich panoply of experience.

Our (thoracic) diaphragm— the dome-shaped sheet of muscle under our ribs—tends to harbor feelings the most, although any place in the body can do so.

In my experience, feelings give us a key to our shackles as well as releasing them, as we will explore in part 3.

BEING IN THE HEART

In alternative circles, people fashionably talk about "being in the heart" or "following your heart."

Recent scientific research has shown that such talk goes beyond New Age Speak.

For example, research by the HeartMath Institute showed that "negative" emotions "threw the nervous system out of sync, and when that happened ... heart rhythms became disordered and appeared jagged on a heart-rhythm monitor." In contrast, "positive" emotions "were found to increase order and balance in the nervous system, and produced smooth, harmonious, sine-wave-like (coherent) heart rhythm," also known as "heart coherence." Such harmonious rhythms reduced stress and also "enhanced people's ability to think more clearly and to self-regulate their emotional responses."[88]

This research supports the hypothesis "that the energetic heart has communication channels connecting it with the physical heart, which then communicates intuitive information to the brain's emotional centers and frontal cortex."

Further HeartMath research has established that heart coherence slows down people's breathing, reduces blood pressure and brain rhythms, quiets the "inner noise" of the brain, resets the amygdala so that the brain becomes less reactive, rebalances the endocrine and immune systems, and increases intuition.[89]

HEART AND ~~SOUL~~ BRAIN

Intuition doesn't preclude logic or reason—using your (left) brain. We have both faculties, so clearly both are useful, complementary.

Alfred Adler is memorably quoted as saying: "Follow your heart but take your brain with you."[90]

PART 3

TOOLS FOR RELEASING SHACKLES

NOTICE, ACKNOWLEDGE, EMBRACE, RELEASE

We tend to assume that everything in our lives is staying the same: what Joe Dispenza calls "the habit of being yourself."[91]

Matrix Energetics encourages us to "Notice what you notice." Then after we play with the energy of a situation, "Notice what's different."

First and foremost, notice what is arising. What are you feeling and where are you feeling it in your body? What thoughts are coming up, especially repetitive ones, or those that are often dismissed as "monkey mind"? What people are swinging into our view? What challenges is life bringing us?

I ask my clients to notice everything that's changing in their lives and write it down for a few days. They are generally astonished by how much is changing — and how fast. This practice helps people to slip into a new and beneficial practice of expecting everything to change.

Notice how the thoughts, feelings, people, and challenges change over time, even over a short time. Life is not as static as we have been trained to believe.

Rather, "everything changes"[92] and "everything is changing" in every moment. Every moment. If we could step back from the moments, we would see the change happening rapidly, as in a time-lapse video.

Whatever is arising, pleasant or painful, acknowledge its presence and allow it to be there, embracing it, without censoring or even needing to name it.

Acknowledgment and embracing immediately change the energy of the situation. No fight-or-flight. No suppression by food or drugs or TV. No escape. No need to escape.

Before long, in my experience, the energy shifts to the point where something recognizably new shows up. A new thought or emotion. An idea. An insight into the situation.

I have noticed that emotions often work in layers. Beneath rage we may find sadness; and beneath that, humiliation; and beneath that, loneliness; and so on. In the bottom layer something supportive may be present, such as fortitude, of which we believed ourselves incapable. If so, then we can connect with that quality at any time. Or perhaps the layers begin again.

At any stage, at any point, in any layer, something can release of its own volition, and we may feel the *qi* shift. Alternatively, the idea that pops up may spur us to action. To move around. To engage with someone whose energy has affected us. To look up something we once read on the subject.

Go with the flow.

TELLING THE TRUTH (TO YOURSELF AND OTHERS)

"How often have I said to you that when you have eliminated the
impossible,
whatever remains, however improbable, must be the truth?"
Sherlock Holmes[93]

Do we have "a" truth and, if so, how do we discover it?

Is our truth different from the truth of Consciousness, or the sum of all
possible perspectives on a situation? In other words, do both relative and
absolute truth exist?

If we simply follow our intuition and tune in to our Heart, will we
always be true?

As Consciousness in human form we live a paradoxical life. We
experience our perspective: thoughts, feelings, beliefs, opinions, hopes, and
desires. In our human form, we own that perspective, speaking of "my"
thoughts, feelings, beliefs, opinions, hopes, and desires. And we can
observe that our perspective changes in time.

We also know from checking in with other people that they profess to
have different feelings, beliefs, opinions, hopes, and desires.

We cannot know the experience of others from the inside, to have first-
hand knowledge of it, only learn about it second-hand.

Even if we have a realization that at some level no separation exists
between us and other people, at the same time we still have an experience
of separation, of individuality, and of relationship with others.

At the human level, we know our thoughts, feelings, beliefs, opinions,
hopes, and desires. And yet, because of conditioning, because of shackles
of all kinds, we may have doubts about the truth of our thoughts, feelings,
beliefs, opinions, hopes, and desires. Then we may defer to the expressed
feelings, beliefs, opinions, hopes, and desires of others, believing them
superior to ours.

Perhaps such deference constitutes the greatest shackle of all.

Yes, of course, we need second-hand knowledge from those to whom
we accord cognitive authority in order to live.

Yet if we don't also live as much as possible from our own feelings,
beliefs, opinions, hopes, and desires — our own first-hand
knowledge — then we are living a second-hand life.

How much life changes when we can say, simply, "This is my

experience," adding, "Please tell me about your experience."

But first, we need to acknowledge and value our own experience, then feel comfortable speaking up about it. After many years of conditioning, of deference, this process takes time, patience, self-love, and self-respect.

At the same time, our own experience may become increasingly colored by intuitions of no separation from others or from Consciousness, by intimations of some greater Truth whose truth we are reflecting.

LIFE FOR FOOD

In part 1, I advocated finding what food suits you: releasing what does not suit you, then finding other food that suits you better.

Inevitably, at first we are going to be influenced by second-hand knowledge: others' ideas about food. So I suggest that you use your intuition, not forgetting your brain, to discover appealing ideas. Then test these ideas out on yourself.

Ask your body, in this moment, does this food suit you now? Even if it suited you last week, does it suit you now? Even if it suits your spouse, even if your family has eaten it for generations, does it suit you now?

Also pay attention to the effect on you of foods, and methods of food preparation, that you are accustomed to. For example — yes, a loaded example — Americans commonly drink ice water with their meals. What effect does the extreme cold have on your body? And are you chewing the food fully, or perhaps washing some of it down?

If a *craving* for some food or drink arises — a strong, perhaps irresistible, desire to eat or drink something in this moment — does it occur at a regular interval, such as the same time each day? That suggests part of the craving is chemical.

Or is strong emotion coming up along with the craving? If you pay attention to the emotion and befriend it, what happens to the craving?

I believe that when we pay attention, now and in every moment, food can truly nourish us, not be another series of shackles.

TOXIC NO MORE

My Rule of Thumb: If we have the slightest suspicion that something is toxic at quantities in which it is found in our environment, no matter how many reassurances corporations, scientists, experts, and governments issue about how safe it is, then sooner or later strong evidence will emerge that it is harmful.

An overstatement? Just consider the reassurances that the American Dental Association is still giving about mercury in dental amalgam after 170 years, despite evidence of the harm it causes.[94] In contrast, Dr. William Virtue, President of the International Academy of Oral Medicine and Toxicology, has written: "While worldwide action is being taken to protect humans and the environment from mercury, the ADA continues to mislead the public into believing that one of the most toxic elements on this planet somehow becomes less poisonous when it is placed in their mouths."[95]

Act now!

Inform yourself.[96]

Stop exposing yourself to such toxins as far as you can.

Learn about how to release the toxins from your body.[97]

And spread the word.

KINESIOLOGY

(Applied) kinesiology is based on the observation that a strong muscle is weakened considerably by certain substances, environmental factors, "negative" thoughts, etc.[98]

As a method of testing for your own truth, does kinesiology really work, or is it just another belief? Scientific research is beginning to show its validity.[99]

In any case, it *appears* to work, and in my experience it's useful until your intuition kicks in.

Here's the one-person version I learned years ago from a book by Machaelle Small Wright:

"The circuit fingers: If you are right-handed, place your left palm up. Connect the tip of your left thumb with the tip of the left little finger....

"If you are left-handed, place your right palm up. Connect the tip of your right thumb with the tip of your right little finger.

"By connecting your thumb and little finger, you have just closed an electrical circuit in your hand....

"The test fingers: ... Place the thumb and index finger of your other hand inside the circle you have created by connecting your thumb and little finger.... Don't try to make a circle with your test fingers.....

"Keeping this position, ask yourself a yes/no question in which you already know the answer to be yes. Once you've asked the question, press your circuit fingers together, keeping the tip-to-tip position. Using the same amount of pressure, try to pull apart the circuit fingers with your test fingers....

"If the answer to the question is positive ... you will not be able to easily pull apart the circuit fingers. The electrical circuit will hold, your muscles will maintain their strength, and your circuit fingers will not separate....

"Once you have a clear sense of the positive response, asking yourself a question that has a negative answer.... This time the electrical circuit will break and the circuit fingers will weaken and separate."[100]

A simplified version uses a circle made by the thumb and middle finger of one hand, and the index or middle finger of the other hand trying to pull the circle apart.

John Diamond describes only a two-person version of kinesiology using the middle part of the receiver's deltoid as the indicator muscle, a version that will be familiar to many readers from visits to the chiropractor or physical therapist. He recommends performing the kinesiology at the beginning of every session, "test-touching" on the subject's thymus point (technically, the sternomanubrial joint on the upper chest where the second rib joins the breastbone); because if that tests weak, all subsequent tests will be invalid. Thumping the thymus point ten or twenty times should reset it, after which the test-touching result should be positive and the rest of the kinesiology can proceed.[101]

LEFT–RIGHT

Here's an exercise I use for reconciling apparent opposites in our being.

Suppose you have a love–hate relationship with your mother. (Sorry, mom, but I need an example. Could be dad or anyone else instead.)

Stand up and hold your arms out in front of you with the palms upwards.

Imagine that your love is in your left hand and your hate is in your right hand. Check your sense of which feeling should be in which hand.

Continue to hold your arms out loosely, so that they can move in any way they like. Also allow your body to move in any way it wants.

Whether your body is moving or not, your hands may stay still, move up or down, spin in circles, cross over each other, cross back, move apart. Whatever happens, happens. Just allow whatever's arising to arise.

If your hands come together in a prayer position and you have a sense of completion, then stop.

If one hand goes down or up and stays there for a few minutes, check if you have a sense of completion about that.

What is your sense of your relationship with loving and hating your mother now? Any change?

"SWIMMING" IN CONSCIOUSNESS

Here's another exercise.

Open your arms wide and connect with Consciousness. Feel, literally feel, that Consciousness is all there is.

Then bring in your arms and put your hands over your heart. Feel that you are Consciousness in human form.

Allow your arms to "swim" out and in, feeling Consciousness, then Consciousness in human form, with every "stroke."

Take something you would like to manifest   By intention, "seed" it into the swimming. Then continue to swim until you have a sense of closure.

A WORD ABOUT WORDS

When directed at us, *should* implies doing or saying something that another person or group believes would be good for us.

When directed at ourselves, the word implies doing or saying something that we have been trained to believe would be good for us.

We should eliminate "should" from our vocabulary. ~~We should~~

"Supposed to" has a similar implication.

Test out the effect of saying "I choose to" rather than "I should," "I'm supposed to," "I have to," or even "I need to."

LAMA

Lama Tantrapa, one of my mentors, coaches Qi Gong rather than teaching it.[102]

The essential difference between the two approaches consists in exploring his suggestions for yourself, to discover what works for you, rather than being told how to do something. No "do's," no "shoulds."

In Lama's approach to Qi Gong, unlike the vast majority of traditional practices, pre-set forms simply don't exist. He points out that forms codify, or make into an institution, the practices of the founders of each branch of the art.

Instead, we allow our bodies to move spontaneously in every moment, becoming the founders of our own Qi Gong.

Working with Lama, I felt vindicated, because I had discovered spontaneous Tai Qi for myself when learning that art a decade earlier. I had given my body permission to move in any way it wanted, nevertheless using the vocabulary of moves I had learned in the forms.

Now I could move even more freely, involving my whole body in every motion. Under Lama's guidance, I found new ways to stand, to walk, to go up and down stairs or inclines, to dance—and to play pool. To my surprise, I even beat him at pool twice in a row.

Lama assigns prime importance to the midline or centerline of the body, an imaginary vertical line from head to toe. By doing simple exercises such as pushing but not shoving a student opponent, you discover that you are stronger when your midline faces the opponent.

But don't take my word for it—do it for yourself.

Parallel approaches are found in the dance world in conscious dance or ecstatic dance, in which people dance in a free manner, often to world music, in a quiet and meditative state, by themselves or linking up with others.[103] Conscious dance differs from ecstatic dance in having an "intention" for the dance of the day, set by a facilitator. In either case, no forms, no rules.

Both types of dance differ from boogieing or club dancing, dancing to pop music, although that has its own freedom.

I'm not decrying pre-set forms in movement or dance, which lead to their own kind of experience. Decrying anything tends to produce another shackle. Rather, I'm inviting you to experience free movement to see what serves you in your life in this and every moment.

YOU WHEN? YOU WIN

In section 2 (p. 47), we took a brief look at energy healing, which offers a powerful way to release many shackles quickly.

Dr. Kam Yuen, the founder of the Yuen Method of energy healing, has come up with the simplest of techniques for releasing anything in our lives that is not serving us.[104] It does require using your intuition first, to determine what needs releasing.

Like Lama Tantrapa, who is part of a similar long lineage of practitioners in the East, Dr. Yuen makes use of the midline of the body.

Keep in mind what you want to release, think of your midline, then send the intention to do the releasing.

Too good to be true? Too easy to be true? Certainly, Dr. Yuen teaches various additions that strengthen the technique, but even the basic version can work.

BODYCHAT

Earlier I cited BodyTalk as a powerful modality of energy healing.

The BodyTalk System®, developed by John Veltheim, is an integrative system of healthcare that incorporates insights from energy medicine, Western medicine, traditional Chinese medicine, and other traditional systems of healing. The system is based on the principle that the body-mind has the innate wisdom to heal itself, but becomes blocked by various influences: physical, mental, emotional, spiritual, and environmental.

BodyTalk uses the practitioner's innate and trained abilities to focus on what parts of the client's body-mind are blocked, then restore communication to them, based on a sequence of priorities determined by the client's innate wisdom. BodyTalk does not diagnose or "treat" in the medical sense, but shifts the client's dynamic balance toward a healthier way of being. It can be performed in person or at a distance.

Some BodyTalk techniques can be picked up from reading the published books and articles on the modality.[105]

But BodyTalk can be learned fully only through taking workshops, in which students are immersed in the BodyTalk matrix, as its morphic field is called.

A quick version of a few of the basic techniques is taught to the public in a one-day workshop under the name BodyTalk Access

Sometimes members of the public become fixated on the "tapping" technique universally employed in BodyTalk, supposing that BodyTalk is therefore similar to other modalities that employ tapping, such as EFT (the Emotional Freedom Technique). It isn't. The tapping ensures that the results of the session are "fixed" in the consciousness of the client.

BodyTalk was endorsed in James Oschman's book *Energy Medicine: The Scientific Basis*, and scientific research on BodyTalk is now underway.[106]

LOVE ME, LOVE ME, LOVE ME

Few children are loved unconditionally, so we end up as adults lacking self-love or worse. Take a look back at Self-X in Part 1 (p. 21).

If you can identify at what age you developed a particular negative attitude towards yourself, imagine your self of that age standing in front of you.[107] Offer the child assistance and ask what she or she would like from you. It may be a hug, comfort, reassurance, acceptance, validation of feelings, to be seen and heard for the first time.

Then, whenever the child comes into your mind again, make the same offer. Be patient, because it may take many sessions over many weeks before the child feels comfortable. Sure, it's a kind of "inner-child" work.

Tribal cultures had ceremonies to initiate their young men and women into adulthood. The Jewish bar mitzvah and bat mitzvah survive from that tradition. Besides those, nowadays we are mostly left with piercings and tattoos.

We can go back and support ourselves, not only to come of age but retrospectively to pass through other critical times, such as the first days of elementary, middle, and high school, moving house, moving to another culture, our first sexual experiences, divorce, and any form of abuse.

I highly recommend Teal Swan's book on how we can learn to love ourselves.[108] Her simplest and most fundamental suggestion: in every challenging situation, ask yourself what someone who loves herself or himself would do.[109] She recommends following this practice every day for a year.

And here's a surprising simple practice, when we believe we can do it.... By intention, send yourself unconditional love. Bask in it for a few minutes. At the very least, it relaxes us, and in my experience it frees us to make a more intuitive response to challenges and decisions.

MATH FOR THE HEART

Here's a simple HeartMath practice to develop heart coherence (see p. 52).

Focus your attention on our heart. Breathe in and out slowly and deeply. Imagine a positive feeling such as appreciation, care, or compassion. Radiate that feeling to yourself and others.[110]

IN-DISPENZA-BLE

Joe Dispenza has mentored scientific research that shows how powerful our intention can be in changing our lives.[111]

When you imagine, or "intend," a different future for yourself, your body starts to make physiological changes immediately, particularly to the neural network. Dispenza punningly refers to this phenomenon as "making your mind matter."

Dispenza has coupled the results of this scientific research with his practical experience that the intention is strengthened considerably when we are in an open meditative state before setting the intention, in which we feel no separation between us and Consciousness, then feel gratitude for the different future. The details and timing of that future are released to Consciousness.

Note that Dispenza's discovery goes beyond "the power of positive thinking" in at least two respects: the meditative state and the positive emotion.

MUTUALITY

Waking Down in Mutuality (now called Trillium Awakening)[112] recognizes the "down" of life (being human) and "mutuality" (relationship) as having equal standing with "waking" (realizing our nature as Consciousness).

The term *Mutuality* may sound a bit academic: functionality for everyone, perhaps? But it's a powerfully simple concept, and simply powerful.[113]

We acknowledge first and foremost that at the level of Radiant Energy, no separation exists between ourselves and others — we are all One.

Nevertheless, in the human dimension, the "down," we all have our own unique path, our own unique perspective, and our own unique timing.

In practicing Mutuality, we acknowledge both the unity and the uniqueness of human beings by respecting the path, perspective, and timing of others. And, just as importantly, we respect our own path, perspective, and timing.

On the practical level of dealing with others, instead of blaming, complaining, criticizing, lecturing, name-calling, asserting that we are right, attacking, or offering unsolicited advice, we can simply express how the other person's words or actions have affected us.

Speak honestly but compassionately. Listen honesty but compassionately to feedback from others about how we have had an impact on them, too.

Everyone wants to be heard and to be seen. Everyone wants us to "hold space" for them.

If someone tells us that our words and actions have hurt them, we can hold ourselves accountable: express regret and make amends.

Seems too Pollyanna? And won't it open us up to abuse?

No, we don't need to take abuse, especially if it threatens our safety. Walk away, if we can, or get help.

And we don't need to forgive anyone until we have fully processed the impact of their words and actions on us.

Mutuality can nurture unshackled communication, connection, and trust.

Does it mean that the person you are speaking to won't get upset or take what you said "the wrong way"? No, in my experience, but at least your end of the conversation feels honest.

NVC

A similar perspective is provided by Nonviolent Communication, which was developed by the psychologist Marshall B. Rosenberg (1934–2015), beginning in the 1960s.[114] According to NVC, something is "violent" when it diminishes our own or others' well-being.

NVC is based on a number of premises that pan out in practice.[115] What if we treat our relationships as if:

• We all have the same universal needs: for physical sustenance, security, autonomy, leisure, affection, mattering, community, understanding, meaning, and transcendence.

• All our actions are attempts to meet our needs. In NVC, actions are called "strategies," which are specific to time, place, and person. For example, "I want *you* [and only you] to go to the movie with me."

• Conflict does not arise at the level of needs, because the number of strategies that can meet needs is unlimited. Rather, conflict arises when your strategy clashes with mine.

• Our feelings let us know whether our needs are being met ("positive" feelings) or not ("negative" feelings).

• Other people's words and actions may be a stimulus of our own feelings, but they are not the cause, which lies in our interpretations.

• All people have the capacity for compassion and are able to learn how to access it.

• We resort to violence, whether verbal or psychological or physical, when we are not connected with compassion to our shared humanity, and/or when one or more of our needs have gone unmet for a long time.

• When we are not connected with compassion to our shared humanity, we are less likely to find effective strategies for meeting our needs.

NVC acknowledges our shared humanity with compassion and dignity. It seeks to understand the needs that underlie our own and others' words or actions, even when those words and actions are violent.

NVC liberates by showing us how to:

• distinguish observations (the facts) from our interpretations, evaluations, and judgements;

• avoid making assumptions about others' intentions, thoughts, feelings, or needs;

• differentiate feelings from thoughts;

• make requests rather than demands;

• in making requests of ourselves or others, be clear and specific, make sure the request can actually be done, and be willing to hear a "no" without feeling upset or resentful;

• empathize with the feelings and needs of ourselves and others that underlie our words and actions;

• understand that "empathy" involves sensing into and acknowledging or (ideally) guessing the feelings and needs someone is experiencing; it's an emotionally involved experience, not an intellectual exercise;

• express appreciation to celebrate, not manipulate;

• receive appreciation with dignity and honesty, neither deflecting the appreciation nor puffing ourselves up.

The principles of NVC can help us release the shackles of violent or "life-alienating" communication and develop our compassion—for others and for ourselves.

THRIVING
by Vika Miller

My friend Vika Miller is a Nonviolent Communication educator, relationship coach, and "happiness researcher" in Portland, Oregon.[116] For this book she has kindly written the following account of her work, which builds on NVC in a way that I find releases even more shackles:

Two of my favorite teachings from NVC are the idea of "making life more wonderful" for ourselves and others, and the encouragement to live from what's most alive in us. For me, "making life more wonderful" is all about thriving, and I believe our inner sense of what feels most alive or right to us is our wisest, most powerful guide.

I call my body of work Thriving Life. It takes my own 40+ years of research and practice and weaves in the wisdom of NVC and the latest neuroscience findings into a very practical, down-to-earth way of developing effective communication, connection, and happiness skills.

Thriving Life recognizes that the universal human needs that NVC identifies are actually *pathways to thriving*. And when we're thriving, we're happy, and our "natural" tendencies to be generous, kind, patient, playful, creative, etc. spontaneously arise in us. The only reason to do anything is because we believe it will help us thrive.

"Feeling safe" — a feeling of physical relaxation and emotional calm — is an essential part of thriving. We feel safe either when our needs are sufficiently met, or when we feel confident, consciously or unconsciously, that our needs for well-being *will* be met in the future.

As NVC notes, our body sensations and feelings are actually guides, letting us know if we're moving towards or away from thriving. When what we need to thrive is missing — that is, when our needs are not being met — we experience uncomfortable, "negative" body sensations and feelings. So physical and emotional discomfort, pain, and especially stress and suffering are like fire alarms: they're our nervous system letting us know, "Hey, we have a problem here! We're going in the wrong direction, away from thriving! Something different needs to happen."

Learning how to thrive starts with learning how to pay attention to and feel what's going on in our bodies, and to identify (name) our feelings. Next, we learn to identify (name) the needs that our body sensations and feelings are telling us are being met or unmet.

Once we can feel our feelings and can identify what we're needing, we can ask ourselves the $64,000 question: "What can I do to better support my thriving *today*? What are some things I could do that might better meet my needs and increase my well-being?"

If we're feeling good because XYZ need(s) *have* been met, we can really enjoy and celebrate that. And we can note and repeat what actually worked to meet those needs and create that well-being we're experiencing.

If, on the other hand, we're feeling discomfort, pain, stress, or suffering because ABC need(s) are *not* being met, we can realize that this empowers us to start trying some things that might better meet our needs. New strategies could include changing what we're telling ourselves, doing something differently, sharing some information with someone, or making a request of ourselves or someone else.... There are many ways of meeting needs and increasing our well-being.

Then we notice how that worked out for us. We pay attention to what we have been doing and to what that has created for us — how it feels in our bodies, how calm and relaxed we feel. If it feels good *and* we feel calm, we're on the right track.

One important note: We need to pay close attention when we feel good *but anxious*. Often this combination means that what feels good in the moment is actually diminishing our well-being, rather than helping it to blossom. Codependent relationships — parent–child, friends, work, romantic — are common places where this good–anxious feeling tends to come up a lot. Our body's sense of calm and relaxation is probably the wisest guide we have for knowing when something is truly good for us

When we start noticing our feelings and the unmet needs they represent, and then try out ways to get those needs met and start noticing what does and doesn't work, then we start moving towards thriving. And in turn our energy, clarity, confidence, and happiness all naturally start increasing, along with our capacity for compassion, generosity, creativity, play, and every other positive human quality and inner experience we can think of.

What could be more worth cultivating than that?

STRESS, UPSETS, WELL-BEING, AND THE 20-SECOND RULE
by Vika Miller

One of our most powerful shackles is being unclear about where our positive and negative feelings are coming from. If we don't understand what's enhancing or diminishing our well-being, how can we make good choices that will help us thrive better?

Most of us have the belief[117] that all the wonderful feelings we have when we're with someone we love are coming from that person. In reality a lot of what feels so good is the lovely parts of *us* they bring alive—parts of us that we ourselves can evoke and experience any time we wish, even if or when that person is no longer in our lives, for whatever reason.

This mistaken belief that we're dependent on others for our "good" experiences, and the accompanying mistaken belief that others are the cause of all the "negative" things we feel in our interactions with them, creates the most profound suffering and even violence in us.

These mistaken beliefs are actually life-threatening, which is probably why they often stimulate such intense upset in us. That's our nervous system letting us know that our well-being is diminishing. The new fields of Interpersonal Neurobiology (IPNB) and Epigenetics have revealed that our feelings and thoughts or beliefs don't just create our emotional experience and well-being. They also shape our brain and impact our cell and organ functioning, our immune system and digestion, and many other aspects of our overall physical health.

We all know that an enormous portion of the stress in our lives comes from difficult interactions and relationships with others. And not long ago, studies clearly established that stress and inflammation are the root cause of most disease.[118] Now recent research is showing that chronic stress affects our bodies' ability to manage the inflammatory response.[119]

So let's look at one of the greatest causes of our stress: our confusion about where the pain in our relationships is coming from.

It's been suggested, and it seems to bear out in experience, that the impact of what we experience dissipates within about 20 seconds—*if* we add nothing to it.

What does this mean when it comes to how we impact each other?

Well, if I angrily yell something at you one time, it's extremely likely that your nervous system is going to go into a certain level of alarm. It's hard-wired to do that.

Let's say I practically never yell at you in anger, and after I angrily yell this one time, I calm down a bit. If you quite literally "don't make anything of that" — if you don't make that mean anything, or tell yourself anything about that, and if you've never had any bad experiences with someone yelling angrily at you before — then after about 20 seconds your nervous-system alarm will dissipate and you'll go back to being calm.

I think we can all agree that I'm responsible for that 20 seconds of hard-wired alarm that your nervous system experienced. I put that energy out there; it was my creation. If other people were within earshot, their nervous systems probably went into hard-wired alarm, too. I'm responsible for all of that impact, as well.

But what happens *after* that 20 seconds isn't my creation. Whatever your past experience with angry yellers might have been, that may have left your nervous system hypersensitive to angry yelling. Whatever you tell yourself it means that I yelled in anger; or however you take in my angry words — none of these are my creation; they are yours to own and manage.

For example, you could tell yourself I'm just like your violent parent. You could tell yourself I'm just tired and overworked. You could tell yourself that it doesn't work for you to be spoken to in that way, and tell me the next time I speak to you that way, our interaction will end, no matter where we are or what we're doing — and then make sure you follow through on that. You could tell yourself my upset was understandable, because you can see why I wouldn't enjoy the thing you did that I was yelling about. There are limitless ways to interpret and respond to any kind of experience.

Far more than the present-moment event itself, it is our interpretations that create what our nervous system experiences right now — whether those interpretations are made up in the present, or carried over from past experiences and added to this current event.

And we are the creator of all that internal stuff, not the person who yelled angrily at us once, or any of those other annoying or upsetting things that *other* people do. (Tongue firmly planted in cheek.)

If you're still not clear that this is true, try out my favorite revelation. Let's say you yell angrily at me about something I did. Your angry yelling lasts, what — maybe 10 seconds?

Then what happens? Well, on a bad day I go and replay that in my mind again and again, angrily telling myself how wrong you were, or trying to figure out how to keep that from happening again, or whatever. I do this for hours. Maybe weeks. Or months. Or even years.

Who is responsible for what I experience (20 seconds) after you're done yelling? I think it's me. I'm the one recreating all that alarm in my nervous system, again and again. In effect, I'm the one who's doing almost all the angry yelling at me. Your angry yelling lasted 10 seconds or a minute; mine lasted years.

So, we need to take great care when we're allocating responsibility for how our words and actions impact each other.

I think the no. 1 cause of pain and upset between human beings is when the "sender" is blamed for what the "receiver" experiences after that first 20 seconds. We seem to have an instinct for when we're being blamed for hurt that we didn't cause, and we pretty reliably respond to that unfair blame with firm defensiveness — while also usually missing that we are indeed responsible for the impact of that first 20 seconds.

These are just a few examples of the illuminating, empowering tools that NVC and IPNB give us for unraveling our upsets with each other, and dealing with the confusion that comes up when our nervous systems become reactive. For more tools for solving the mystery of your "people problems" and building your thriving skills, visit www.thrivinglifenvc.org.

THE HYPERMASCULINE

From Trillium Awakening comes another useful insight: the hypermasculine. This macho-sounding compound refers to the notion that anything and everything in life can be fixed, improved, and developed.

TA's approach encourages us to let go of compulsive improvement and allow "The Rot" of everyday life to take us where it may.

But isn't that antithetical to releasing your shackles?

Not necessarily: it can be similar to "The Rot" if the shackles are released as, and only as, they come to us to be released—no "pushing the river."[120]

Can we release our shackles completely? Probably not. But as every shackle releases, we become freer.

UNSCHOOLING

> "All human beings by nature desire to know."
> The opening sentence of Aristotle, *Metaphysica* (fourth century BC)[121]

Unschooling means that, instead of following a curriculum, divided into academic subjects, children are trusted to learn whatever they are naturally inclined to learn relevant to their own lives, at their own speed, in their own learning style, according to their intrinsic motivation, and developing self-reliance, while mixing with people of all ages rather than being segregated by age.[122] Their parents act not as all-knowing authorities but as facilitators, providing support, feedback, and resources, discussing the ramifications of whatever is arising, and looking out for the child's safety.

Whatever is learned when children want or need knowledge tends to be remembered and understood naturally, because children grasp how that knowledge fits and connects with what they have already absorbed.[123] No need for rote memorization and regurgitation.

Unschooling emerged out of homeschooling (teaching our children at home rather than sending them to school).[124] I concede that it's an unlovely label.... So call it "natural learning" or "life learning" if you wish.[125]

The unschooling approach need not preclude children taking individual lessons or classes, being tutored, joining learning groups, going on collective field trips, doing part-time work, starting their own businesses, or anything else that fosters the child's learning and needs of the moment.

An initial period of *deschooling* is common in which unschooling may not be followed completely while both child and parents begin to release the shackles of being oriented solely towards schooling and start to explore what the child is naturally interested in.[126]

You might suspect unschooling to be a recipe for anarchy, in which illiterate urchins end up acting out *Lord of the Flies* or playing video games day and night while subsisting on microwaved frozen pizza.[127] Yes, these are extreme cases I invented to make a point, but the fear about video games has often been brought up to me as an objection.

Evidence suggests that, within the feedback of a supportive family setting, unschooling tends to bring out the natural best in children.[128] Peter Gray even provides evidence that playing video games can be highly beneficial, provided opportunities also exist for children to play outdoors.[129]

Unschooling isn't a cop out for children. Working through the frustrations inherent in learning anything worthwhile, and making informed choices, also teaches patience, persistence, fortitude, and resourcefulness.

"Wait, wait!" I hear you cry. "Doesn't society have a body of knowledge that it needs to impart to all its citizens? And doesn't that knowledge require a somewhat standardized curriculum?"

Think back to your own education (unless you were unschooled). Beyond a basic literacy in language and math, and what you need for your current profession, how much of the knowledge that was so rigorously impressed on you through testing and grading have you retained to this day?

And think of subjects you were inspired to learn by yourself. Have you retained more or less? Of course, this is an (un)academic question....

Although adults have probably never thought of "lifelong learning" as unschooling, when they have finished their formal schooling they tend to learn in a more flexible way: from a combination of lessons, classes, relatives, friends, colleagues, reading, videos, websites, and trial-and-error on the task. Unschooling extends the concept of lifelong learning back to the beginning of life.

UNSCHOOL?

Could anything akin to "unschooling" work at school? Certainly, it would be challenging to find even an adequate surrogate for the support of a loving family.

Summerhill School in England, founded in A. S. Neill in 1924 and still going today, paved the way in breaking down the barriers between teachers and students, making classes optional, and allowing students to learn at their own pace, no matter how glacial.[130]

In the United States, the Sudbury Valley School in Framington, Massachusetts (SVS), founded in 1968 by Daniel Greenberg, a private school with low tuition rates, takes children from pre-school through high school.[131] The students learn whatever they like, without a curriculum. When students request classes, they are offered for as long as the need exists. SVS has no "teachers," only adult staff members, who have one-year contracts, then must be re-elected. They serve as the adult members of the community, ensuring safety and comfort, protecting, doing chores, and serving as resources. SVS is run by all the students and staff members, one-person-one-vote, based on a weekly School Meeting. The Meeting makes its own rules, enforced by a Judicial Committee of students and one staff member, who have the power to sentence those found "guilty" of violating the rules to mild consequences. The democratic and judicial aspects of SVS are clearly different from a family setting. The students are free to move about the building and 10-acre campus all day, 8:30 am to 5:00 pm, and venture off-campus with certain provisos. Books, computers, and equipment to support learning are widely available. Students at SVS become knowledgeable, articulate, self-motivated, critical thinkers, able converse readily with people of all ages; they develop deep relationship, love the outdoors, engage with ethical issues, and learn quickly. About eighty percent go on to college, where the qualities they have developed stand them in good stead.

More than three dozen schools around the world, known as "Sudbury schools," now use the same approach.[132]

Could an unschooling approach be successful for college, especially for learning the large body of knowledge needed for working in certain professions? Independent Study and Individualized Majors give us an idea of how to move in that direction. Some elements of a model are provided by Antioch College in Yellow Springs, Ohio, which pioneered self-designed majors, study abroad, interdisciplinary study, and portfolio evaluation, and alternates classroom and work experience ("Cooperative Education").[133]

Similarly, Prescott College in Arizona strives to be "Unplugged from such conventional practices as the departmentalization of knowledge, confining learning to the classroom and textbooks rather than real experience, and thinking of college as preparation for life, rather than life itself. An organic process, moving almost seamlessly between teachers and students, focused on questions and problems that matter deeply to both. Prescott students learn critical thinking and research and how to apply them to real-life problems and their own passions by living them and testing them out in real time."[134]

How many students need the college format, even a modified one, for what they want to learn? In the business world, at least, trial-and-error on the job — their own job — has worked well for some of the most successful people in the world.[135]

PARENTING REVISITED

In parallel with unschooling a style of parenting exists in which parents:

• see themselves as their children's allies or partners rather than masters;

• work together as a team with their children, so everyone has input, and everyone can express their needs without manipulation or power trips;[136]

• allow their children to experience the natural consequences of their actions, behavior, and decisions, rather than using reward and punishment;

• nurture their children's self-motivation and self-regulation.[137]

The most important characteristic of the parent–child relationship, as in every relationship, is connection. As Shefali Tsabary remarks, cutely and astutely: "All children yearn for connection—not correction."[138] I would add that they also yearn for respect.

In my experience, this style of parenting can create an unprecedented closeness among parents and children.

Recent research suggests that children who grow up to be creative come from families with far fewer rules.[139] Their parents emphasize children developing their own moral values and finding joy in their work.

Parenting revisited imposes far fewer shackles than usual on children.

And, as I have discovered myself, it has the side-benefit of releasing *parents'* shackles. To release being controlling feels just as powerful as to release being controlled.

(Yes, another blank page.)

MORPHIC RELEASE BEGGARS BELIEF

Our lives are made up of countless morphic fields. Morphogenetic fields hold us in physical form. And other kinds of morphic fields hold us in mental, emotional, spiritual, social, and cultural form, too.

When that form serves us in the present, then our lives are "in the flow." When any of that form no longer serves us, when it no longer has resonance with the circumstances of our lives, then our energy and our lives become blocked and restricted. We are in shackles.

You cannot get rid of morphic fields: they persist for ever, no matter how weak or strong they are. And a moment's reflection shows that each morphic field is an almost infinite series of frames, going back to birth (and before?). We have morphic resonance not just with the morphic field in general, but with every "frame" of that field, albeit in decreasing strength as we go backwards.

We can release at least some of our morphic resonance with the morphic fields that are no longer serving us. I abbreviate that in my notes as MRNLS (morphic resonance no longer serving). And it needs to be morphic resonance with every "frame" of those fields, from the point where we developed morphic resonance with them to the present.

Finally, after the release, we can strengthen morphic resonance with other morphic fields that serve us now. For example, the morphic field of responding based on the flow of life.

VERSO

I have been identifying morphic fields that are no longer serving my clients, then releasing whatever resonance the clients have with those fields that no longer serves them. To identify the morphic fields in question, I listen to the clients' story, ask questions, and also use my intuition to read the clients' energy. Then I have a number of energy techniques I know that release resonance with morphic fields.

My experience of working with clients suggests that when they book an appointment with me, some of their shackles are ready to be released. I certainly don't have the sense that *I* am releasing anything; but rather, that I am Radiant Energy's agent of release at the right time.

Many of these fields are beliefs that form part of childhood conditioning.

Our parents tell us repeatedly that what we are doing is not good enough, so we develop the belief "I am not good enough." This is a common one. People who are abused as children develop beliefs such as "I am a victim." One of my clients who was punished a lot as a child: "I cannot be fully myself without being hit or shouted at."

"I have an aversion to the cold."

And one from a three-year-old boy whose mother had developed sore nipples: "I cannot fall asleep without breast feeding."

A couple of beliefs from a woman who was lonely as a child: "Nobody cares about me" and "I cannot speak for myself." Another woman: "When a man is around, I feel the need to cater to him." A musician: "There's no money to be made in music." Someone who was struggling in life: "Life is a struggle." Someone who was brought up in a religious culture that found sex problematic: "Sexuality is sinful."

These are not just individual beliefs but associated with strong *morphic fields* with which the millions or even billions of people have morphic resonance. Releasing the individual belief does have benefit. But I have found that releasing the person's morphic resonance with the *morphic field* of the belief in addition is much more powerful.

Now, other kinds of morphic fields exist besides belief systems. For example:

A client who lives in Boston and was feeling the effect of the bombs set off during the Boston Marathon in 2013: the morphic fields of local, national, and international reaction to the bombs.

A woman who had a turbulent life: regret for the past.

Two different women who were born in the same East European country that had a history of being repressed by Russia: the felt need to fight everything in life.

Many kinds of *fear* are common: fear of letting go of your old self, fear of feeling too good, fear of getting better, fear of change, fear of death, fear of losing your security, fear of the past, fear of the present, fear of the future, fear of punishment, fear of failure, fear of not being good enough, fear of success, fear of enjoyment, fear of responsibility, fear of being hurt, fear of the unknown, fear of missing out, fear of pain, fear of darkness, and fear of going to hell.

In relationships, fear of rejection, fear of abandonment, fear of intimacy, fear of commitment, fear of abuse, and fear of love.

About money, fear of losing money, even fear of making money, fear of poverty, and fear of abundance.

About health, fear of aging, fear of immortality, fear of being too old, and fear of growing old.

So many kinds of fear. And remember: these are not just personal fears; they are also associated with strong morphic fields with which millions of people have had morphic resonance over hundreds or thousands of years.

For groups, I have worked on some morphic fields that we probably all have morphic resonance with but are no longer serving us. For example, the (meta-)morphic field of continuing to have morphic resonance with morphic fields that no longer serve us. Or the morphic field of reacting to our lives based on our childhood conditioning.

DE-CLUTTER YOURSELF

Our possessions reflect what we have accumulated along life's journey — who we have been in the past.

Possessions that no longer serve us in the present clutter and block the flow of energy in our dwellings and in ourselves.

The KonMari method of de-cluttering developed by Marie Kondo is based on a simple principle: keep only those possessions that "spark joy" in you in the present.[140] Then you are surrounded by things you love.[141]

Difficulty in letting possessions go reflects "an attachment to the past or a fear for the future."[142]

Ultimately, "The question of what you want to own is actually the question of how you want to live your life" — now.[143]

I love Eleanor Brownn's extension of "clutter" to whatever is no longer serving you, whether possessions or anything else in your life: "Are you living in a museum? And I don't just mean with your physical stuff. Change is constant. You're not the same person you were even 5 seconds ago. Look around you. Is this a reflection of who you are today, or is it a collection of remnants from the past? And what about old hurts and resentments? Holding onto those, too? It may be time for a thorough housecleaning."[144]

LIFE AS IMPROVISATION

I know a jazz singer who wrote a memoir entitled *Improvisation as a Way of Life*. What a wonderful title, which rings truer to me every day.

In improvising, whether in music or theatre or poetry or life, we make use of known elements, a vocabulary from the past, form from the past. But from the known arises the unknown, a uniquely new creation.[145]

Life is more like an improvisation than a composition. And even compositions have a performance tradition of interpretations, arrangements, and "covers" that reflect the insights and taste of performers who come afterwards.

The more open we are to what is arising, releasing the elements from the past that no longer serve us, the more creative our improvisation, or our performance, will be.

Life is living through us and evolving through us. May we enjoy our improvisation.

CO-CREATION

A friend who lives in Saudi Arabia tells me that she finds the drivers there crazy. They speed. They don't signal. To turn right, they cut across from the left lane without looking. And they never worry about the consequences, because everything is the Will of Allah. I live, it's the Will of Allah. I die, it's the Will of Allah.

Such a belief system belies the role that creativity plays in our lives as Consciousness manifesting in human form and living through us, commonly called "co-creation."

Being creative means releasing beliefs and practices of the past and discovering new territory. It can, but does not have to, imply producing a new object or work of art.

FREE TO PLAY

In play, free play, being playful, we are motivated by the activity itself, not by external reward separate from the activity.[146]
Unschooling is free play.
Parenting revisited is free play.
Improvising is free play (sure, we can also do it for a living).
Co-creating is free play.
Releasing your shackles is free play.

GRATITUDE

We bring many challenges on ourselves, many more shackles, by resisting our experience.

When life is going "well," when pleasant things are happening to us, when "good" feelings are arising, we start to relax and to let go of our resistance. Wow, life is a beach!

But when life starts to go "badly," when unpleasant things happen, when "bad" feelings arise, we tighten up, we resist our resistance, and we may even blame ourselves for resisting the resistance, adding another layer to the tension. Wow, life is a bitch!

So here's the clincher: What if we feel unconditional love and gratitude for everything that is arising in our lives?

Yes, I mean *everything*.

Gratitude for our fears, all of them.

Gratitude for our anger, all of it.

Gratitude for our shame, all of it.

Gratitude for blaming ourselves.

Gratitude for our judgment, all of it.

Gratitude for believing we had to be perfect.

Gratitude for our resistance, all of it.

Gratitude for our difficulty feeling gratitude.

Down, down, down, down the layers.

So start practicing now. Feel unconditional love for everything and everybody in your life. Feel gratitude for everything that is arising in your life in every moment.

Yes, *every*thing and *every*body in *every* moment.

Can you dig it?

"But what if I can't feel gratitude for my emotions or my resistance?"

Feel gratitude for *something*, then seed your emotions or your resistance into that.

THANKS

As we release our shackles, we may realize how much we have learned from having them: what qualities of character we developed, such as patience and fortitude; what sympathy we gained for other people's shackles; what respect we acquired for the human condition.

As we release our shackles, they become our wisdom.[147]

IN SUM

As Rousseau put it 350 years ago, "Human beings are born free, and everywhere they are in shackles." These figurative shackles weaken or block our energy and hinder us from learning who we are, finding our truth in every moment, and living from that truth.

Many of our shackles originate in attempts by others—family, school, church, society—to control us into being like them, not like ourselves.

If we don't know who we are and what we need, then we will tend to swallow what we have been told, developing belief systems that don't serve us and drag us down. Our relationships will become contentious. We won't know what food would be beneficial for us to consume, and we won't notice that we are gradually being poisoned by the environment.

Although we may never feel completely free to be ourselves, we can certainly become much freer. Much.

The road of freedom opens up more easily when we observe and acknowledge just how we have become shackled and understand the power we have as children of Consciousness to free ourselves.

If we don't exactly "create our reality," in the popular sense, we do, both individually and collectively, co-create our reality with Consciousness.

We cannot control life; we cannot "fix" our lives. Yet when we release our resistance to what is arising—and our resistance to our resistance—our hopes, needs, wants, and desires can open up windows into Consciousness that bring in continual surprise.

Although we cannot help but absorb "second-hand knowledge" from others, some of which may indeed be serving us, we can still take every opportunity to discover our own "first-hand knowledge," subjective knowledge, based on feelings, intuition, and feedback from experience.

At the same time, we can refine our skill in seeking and assessing second-hand knowledge, learning how better to sift the (non-GMO) wheat from the chaff.

"Objective" knowledge, science, as useful as it may be, cannot be considered definitive. Rather, scientific theories are adjusted or replaced as time goes by, usually with enormous resistance, based on new evidence and new ways of conceiving reality.

Nevertheless, the quantum theory that originated in the early twentieth century and more recent theories about the Zero Point Field point strongly towards ways of liberation that parallel the experience of mystics for a few thousand years and can be confirmed through our own experience.

The world exists only in potential until consciousness brings it into reality.

By force of comfortable habit, by dint of morphic fields, the world tends to come into reality *almost* the same way in every moment.

The *almost* is the wiggle room, the room for creativity — the room for Consciousness, assisted by *our* consciousness, to introduce a different reality in *this* moment.

Some methods of freeing ourselves stem from simply noticing how we are shackled, then making different choices: for example, avoiding weakening things such as toxins, or becoming stronger by choosing words that release control, or taking in nourishment of all kinds that truly serves us, or dancing and moving naturally, or learning how to love ourselves unconditionally.

When it comes to healing our bodies and our psyches, we can learn techniques to help us based on simple but powerful principles: the body has an innate ability to heal itself; everything is connected; everything changes and is changing; the body's midline is key to strength and intention; intention backed by gratitude is powerful. The helping hand of other people who embody these principles may also be beneficial.

Most of our shackles are not only individual to us, but common to millions or billions of people living in the past or present. Therefore we need to release not only our individual perceptions or beliefs but also morphic resonance with the morphic fields that are no longer serving us.

As parents and teachers, we can find ways of bringing up children that honor and respect their natural inclination to learn what they need to learn for their lives and to discover who they are.

With everyone, we can find ways of relating that honor and respect both their perspective and ours, their feelings and ours, their needs and ours, their thriving and ours.

Life can be great free play, a grand and limitless improvisation, building on the past and heading out into new creative territory. When we are paying attention, we may come to notice that in life, unlike in music, there are no repeats.

Let me repeat that: life has no repeats. Ponder that for a moment.

Ultimately, our shackles present us with opportunities to learn and to grow. Let us be grateful, even as we release the shackles and release more.

Life is living through you.
Life is playing through you,
in a way that's uniquely yours.
Come out to play.
Release your shackles.

WRITINGS CITED

Anthony, Marcus T. "Representations of Integrated Intelligence within Classical and Contemporary Depictions of Intelligence and their Educational Implications." Ph.D. diss., The University of the Sunshine Coast, Australia, 2006.

— — —. "Sheldrake & the Credibility Issue in Modern Science." http://www.mind-futures.com/crisis-in-science/; accessed 8 February 2016.

— — —. "The 12 Secrets of Profound Intuition." Available from http://www.mind-futures.com/intuition/; accessed 20 February 2016.

Aristotle. *The Complete Works of Aristotle, The Revised Oxford Translation.* 2 vols. Edited by Jonathan Barnes. Bollingen Series LXXI. Princeton: Princeton University Press, 1984.

Bartlett, Richard. *Matrix Energetics: The Science and Art of Transformation.* New York: Atria Books; Hillsboro, OR: Beyond Words, 2007.

— — —. *The Physics of Miracles: Tapping into the Field of Consciousness Potential.* New York: Atria Books; Hillsboro, OR: Beyond Words, 2009.

Bergson, Henri. *Creative Evolution.* Translated by Arthur Mitchell. New York: Henry Holt, 1911. Reprint, Mineola, NY: Dover, 1998.

Bly, Robert. *The Sibling Society.* Reading, MA: Addison-Wesley, 1996.

Bogart, Julie. "Why I Gave up the Unschooling Label," http://blog.bravewriter.com/2007/10/12/un-defining-unschooling/; "Explaining Natural Learning," http://blog.bravewriter.com/2016/02/25/explaining-natural-learning-to-your-kids/. Both accessed 26 February 2016.

Bohannon, John. "Who's Afraid of Peer Review? A Spoof Paper Concocted by *Science* Reveals Little or no Scrutiny at Many Open-access Journals." *Science* 342, no. 6154 (4 October 2013): 60–65. DOI: 10.1126/science.342.6154.60.

Bryson, Christopher. *The Fluoride Deception.* New York: Seven Stories Press, 2004.

Cherniske, Stephen. *Caffeine Blues: Wake up to the Hidden Dangers of America's #1 Drug.* New York: Warner Books, 1998.

Childre, Doc, Howard Martin, Deborah Rozman, and Rollin McCraty. *Heart Intelligence: Connecting with the Intuitive Guidance of the Heart.* ([Cardiff, CA]: Waterfront Press, 2016).

Conan Doyle, Arthur. *The Sign of the Four.* Philadelphia: J. B. Lippincott,

1890.

Connett, Paul, James Beck, and H. S. Micklem. *The Case Against Fluoride: How Hazardous Waste Ended up in Our Drinking Water and the Bad Science and Powerful Politics that Keep it There.* White River Junction, VT: Chelsea Green Publishing, 2010.

Dawkins, Richard. *The Selfish Gene.* Oxford & New York: Oxford University Press, 1976.

Descartes, René. *Discours de la méthode* (1637). Version numérique par Jean-Marie Tremblay (2002). Translated as *A Discourse on Method.* Translated by John Veitch. Everyman's Library, 570. London: J. M. Dent; New York: Dutton, [1912].

Diamond, John. *Life Energy: Using the Meridians to Unlock the Hidden Power of Your Emotions.* New York: Dodd, Mead, 1985; St. Paul, MN: Paragon House, 1995.

— — —. *Your Body Doesn't Lie: Unlock the Power of Your Natural Energy.* New York: Warner Books, 1980. Originally published as *BK — Behavioral Kinesiology: How to Activate Your Thymus and Increase Your Life Energy.* New York: Harper & Row, 1979.

Diamond, Nina L. *Purify Your Body: Natural Remedies for Detoxing from 50 Everyday Situations.* New York: Crown Trade Paperbacks, 1996,

Dispenza, Joe. *Breaking the Habit of Being Yourself: How to Lose Your Mind and Create a New One.* Carlsbad, CA: Hay House, 2012.

— — —. *You Are the Placebo: Making Your Mind Matter.* Carlsbad, CA: Hay House, 2014.

Druker, Steven M. *Altered Genes, Twisted Truth: How the Venture to Genetically Engineer Our Food Has Subverted Science, Corrupted Government, and Systematically Deceived the Public.* Salt Lake City, UT: Clear River Press, 2015.

Dufty, William. *Sugar Blues.* Radnor, PA: Chilton Book Co., 1975; New York: Warner Books, 1976.

Ellsberg, Michael. *The Education of Millionaires: Everything You Won't Learn in College about How To Be Successful.* Updated with a new afterword. New York: Portfolio/Penguin, 2012.

Fitzgerald, Randall. *The Hundred-Year Lie: How Food and Medicine Are Destroying Your Health.* New York: Dutton, 2006. Paperback ed. as *The Hundred-Year Lie: How to Protect Yourself from the Chemicals that Are Destroying Your Health.* New York: Plume, 2007.

Gatto, John Taylor. *Weapons of Mass Instruction: A Schoolteacher's Journey*

Lasocki, Release Your Shackles

through the Dark World of Compulsory Schooling. Gabriola Island, BC, Canada: New Society, 2010.

Grant, Adam. "How to Raise a Creative Child. Step One: Back Off." *New York Times,* 30 January 2016. Available from http://www.nytimes.com/2016/01/31/opinion/sunday/how-to-raise -a-creative-child-step-one-back-off.html?smprod=nytcore-ipad&smid=n ytcore-ipad-share&_r=0; accessed 20 February 2016.

— — —. *Originals: How Non-Conformists Move the World.* New York: Viking, 2016.

Gray, Peter. *Free to Learn: Why Unleashing the Instinct to Play Will Make Our Children Happier, More Self-Reliant, and Better Students for Life.* New York: Basic Books, 2013.

— — —, and David Chanoff. "Democratic Schooling: What Happens to Young People who Have Charge of their Own Education?" *American Journal of Education* 94, no. 2 (February 1986): 182–213.

Griffith, Mary. *The Unschooling Handbook: How to Use the Whole World as Your Child's Classroom.* New York: Three Rivers Press, 1998.

Gunnars, Kris. "Modern Nutritional Policy Is Based on Lies and Bad Science." http://authoritynutrition.com/modern-nutrition-policy-lies-bad-scienc e/; accessed 2 February 2016.

Holt, John, and Pat Farenga. *Teach Your Own: The John Holt Book of Home Schooling.* Cambridge, MA: Da Capo Press, 2003,

Horton, Robert. "Offline: What is Medicine's 5 Sigma?" *The Lancet* 385 (11 April 2015): 1380.

Hyman, Mark. *The Blood Sugar Solution 10-Day Detox Diet: Activate Your Body's Natural Ability to Burn Fat and Lose Weight Fast.* New York: Little, Brown, 2014.

Illich, Ivan. *Deschooling Society.* New York: Harper & Row, 1971.

Jensen, Anne. "The Accuracy and Precision of Kinesiology-style Manual Muscle Testing: Designing and Implementing a Series of Diagnostic Test Accuracy Studies." D.Phil. thesis, University of Oxford, 2014. For the abstract, see http://ora.ox.ac.uk/objects/uuid:4fd95394-e812-402e-9195-6c82643eaa1 5; accessed 28 April 2016.

Jerome, Frank J. *Tooth Truth: A Patient's Guide to Metal-Free Dentistry.* Updated edition. Chula Vista, CA: New Century Press, 2000.

Jonsson, Melissa Joy. *M-Joy Practically Speaking: Matrix Energetics and Living*

Your Infinite Potential. Encinitas, CA: M-Joy of Being, 2013.

Journal of Alternative Medicine Research 3, no. 3 (2011). Issue devoted to BodyTalk.

Kendrick, Malcolm. *The Great Cholesterol Con: The Truth about What Really Causes Heart Disease and How to Avoid it.* London: John Blake, 2007.

Kondo, Marie. *The Life-Changing Magic of Tidying Up: The Japanese Art of Decluttering and Organizing.* Translated by Cathy Hirano. Berkeley, CA: Ten Speed Press, 2014.

Laricchia, Pam. *Free to Learn: Five Ideas for a Joyful Unschooling Life.* Erin, Ontario, Canada: Living Joyfully Enterprises, 2012.

Leigh, CC. *Becoming Divinely Human: A Direct Path to Embodied Awakening.* Portland, OR: Wolfsong Press, 2012.

Lo, Shui Yin. *The Biophysics Basis for Acupuncture and Health.* Pasadena, CA: Dragon Eye Press, 2004.

Lowe, Carrie A., and Michael B. Eisenberg. "Big6™ Skills for Information Literacy." In *Theories of Information Literacy*, edited by Karen E. Fisher, Sanda Erdelez, and Lynne (E. F.) McKechnie, ed., 63–68. ASSIST Monograph Series. Medford, NJ: Published for the American Society for Information Science and Technology by Information Today, 2005.

Martin, Dayna. *Radical Unschooling: A Revolution Has Begun.* Rev. ed. Madison, NH: author, 2009.

McTaggart, Lynne. *The Field: The Quest for the Secret Force of the Universe.* London: HarperCollins, 2001; New York: HarperCollins, 2002; New York: Harper Perennial, 2003.

Nachmanovitch, Stephen. *Free Play: Improvisation in Life and Art.* Los Angeles: Jeremy P. Tarcher, 1990.

Neill, A. S. *"Neill! Neill! Orange Peel!": An Autobiography.* New York: Hart, 1972.

Neufeld, Gordon, and Gabor Maté. *Hold on to Your Kids: Why Parents Need to Matter more than Peers.* New York: Ballantine Books, 2005.

Nietzsche, Friedrich. *The Twilight of the Idols and The Anti-Christ.* Translated by R. J. Hollingdale, introduction by Michael Tanner. London: Penguin Books, 1990.

Ohsawa, George. *Zen Macrobiotics: The Art of Rejuvenation and Longevity.* Revised, edited and annotated by Lou Oles. Los Angeles: Ohsawa Foundation, 1965.

Oschman, James L. *Energy Medicine: The Scientific Basis.* Second edition. Edinburgh & New York: Elsevier, 2016. First edition, 2000.

Park, Robert. *Voodoo Science: The Road from Foolishness to Fraud.* Oxford & New York: Oxford University Press, 2000.

Rosenberg, Marshall B. *Nonviolent Communication: A Language of Life.* 3rd edition. Encinitas, CA: PuddleDancer Press, 2015.

Rosenblum, Bruce, and Fred Kuttner. *Quantum Enigma: Physics Encounters Consciousness.* Oxford & New York: Oxford University Press, 2006.

Rousseau, Jean-Jacques. *Du contrat social; ou, Principes du droit politique.* Amsterdam, 1762.

Sheldrake, Rupert. *Morphic Resonance: The Nature of Formative Causation.* 4th revised and expanded US edition. Rochester, VT: Park Street Press, 2009.

– – –. *The Presence of the Past: Morphic Resonance and the Memory of Nature.* Revised and expanded edition. Rochester, VT: Park Street Press, 2012.

– – –. *The Rebirth of Nature: The Greening of Science and God.* Rochester, VT: Park Street Press, 1994.

– – –. "The Replicability Crisis in Science," Available from http://sciencesetfree.tumblr.com/; accessed 8 February 2016.

– – –. *Science Set Free: 10 Paths to New Discovery.* New York: Deepak Chopra Books, 2012.

Shields, David, and Elizabeth Cooperman. *Life is Short – Art is Shorter: In Praise of Brevity.* Portland, OR: Hawthorne Books & Literary Arts, 2014.

Souza, Russell J. de, Andrew Mente, Adriana Maroleanu, Adrian I. Cozma, Vanessa Ha, Teruko Kishibe, Elizabeth Uleryk, Patrick Budylowski, Holger Schünemann, Joseph Beyene, and Sonia S. Anand. "Intake of Saturated and Trans Unsaturated Fatty Acids and Risk of All Cause Mortality, Cardiovascular Disease, and Type 2 Diabetes: Systematic Review and Meta-Analysis of Observational Studies." *BMJ* 2015; 351; doi: http://dx.doi.org/10.1136/bmj.h3978 (published 12 August 2015).

Stebbins, Leslie F. *Finding Reliable Information Online: Adventures of an Information Sleuth.* Lanham, MD: Rowman & Littlefield, 2015.

Stevens, Barry. *Don't Push the River (It Flows by Itself).* ([Lafayette, CA: Real People Press, 1970]).

Stuve, Laura L., Honghu Liu, Jie Shen, Jill Gianettoni, and Janet Galipo. "Evaluation of Body-Talk, a Novel Mind–Body Medicine, for Chronic Pain Treatment." *Journal of Pain Management* 7, no. 4 (2015): 279–90.

Swan, Teal. *Shadows before Dawn: Finding the Light of Self-love through Your Darkest Times.* Carlsbad, CA: Hay House, 2015.

Taubes, Gary, and Cristin Kearns Couzens. "Big Sugar's Sweet Little

Lies—How the Industry Kept Scientists from Asking: Does Sugar Kill?" *Mother Jones*, November/December 2012. Available from http://www.motherjones.com/environment/2012/10/sugar-industry-lies-campaign; accessed 26 February 2016.

Tsabary, Shefali. *Out of Control: Why Disciplining Your Child Doesn't Work … and What Will.* Vancouver, BC, Canada: Namaste, 2013.

Veltheim, John. *BodyTalk Access: A New Path to Family and Community Health.* Sarasota, FL: International BodyTalk Association, 2008.

———. *The BodyTalk System: The Missing Link to Optimum Health.* Sarasota, FL: PaRama, 1999.

———. *The Science and Philosophy of BodyTalk: Healthcare Designed by Your Body.* Sarasota, FL: International BodyTalk Association, 2013.

Vita, Enza. *Always Already Free: Recognizing the Natural Wakefulness that We Were Born with.* Highbury, SA, Australia: Baraka Publishing, 2015.

Wilber, Ken. *The Marriage of Sense and Soul: Integrating Science and Religion.* New York: Random House, 1998.

Wilson, Edward O. *Consilience: The Unity of Knowledge.* New York: Alfred A. Knopf, 1998; New York: Vintage Books, 1999.

Wilson, Patrick. *Second-Hand Knowledge: An Inquiry into Cognitive Authority.* Contributions in Librarianship and Information Science, 44. Westport, CT: Greenwood Press, 1983.

Wolford, DaNelle. "How to Learn all Subjects through Unschooling," http://www.weedemandreap.com/learn-subjects-unschooling/. Accessed 26 February 2016.

Wright, Machaelle Small. *Flower Essences: Reordering Our Understanding and Approach to Illness and Health.* Jeffersonton, VA: Perelandra, 1988.

Yudkin, John. *Pure, White, and Deadly: How Sugar Is Killing us and What We Can Do to Stop it.* Revised edition. New York: Penguin Books, 2013. First published as *Sweet and Dangerous.* New York: Peter H. Wyden, 1972.

Yuen, Kam. *Instant Pain Elimination: How to Stop the Pain You Feel in 2 Minutes or Less.* Canoga Park, CA: CEM Publishers, 2003.

———, and Marnie Greenberg. *Delete Stress and Pain on the Spot!* Henderson, NV: Motivational Press, [2015].

ACKNOWLEDGMENTS

I couldn't possibly mention (or remember) all the authors, colleagues, clients, relatives, and friends who have unwittingly contributed to this book with their ideas and support over my seven decades.

Nevertheless, I would like to acknowledge those people who graciously read or discussed drafts, made suggestions for improvement and expansion, helped me to trace or translate quotations, or just said how much they liked the book: the late Gilly Adkins, Ron Albes, Philippe Allain-Dupré, Sandra Amiry, Janet Barrett, Paul Bullock, Carl Ferré, Nicole Freed, David Gravelle, Krishna Gauci, Jim Johnson, Fred Kuttner, Maryam Larki, Pam Larricchia, Janet Lawson, Betty Bang Mather, Vika Miller, Kristiane Ravn Frost, Alice Sheu, Valerie St. John, Lama Tantrapa, Fern Thornhill, Elaine Turczynski, Lynn Waickman, Tamiko Warren, and members of the Portland Unschoolers group on Facebook.

The material on morphic fields was originally commissioned for a teleseminar I gave for Tantra Maat's Creator Network in September 2013.

My wife Lilin Chen and our son Lucien Lasocki have long supported the project by being themselves.

Laura Serrano Silva created the cover for this book, as for all the Instant Harmony books so far.

My deepest gratitude to one and all.

ABOUT THE AUTHOR

David Lasocki (b. 1947) grew up in Manchester, England. After (barely) completing a B.Sc. degree in chemistry at University College London, he came to the United States in 1969 to attend graduate school in music at The University of Iowa. After amassing entirely too many graduate degrees, including a Ph.D. in musicology (1983), not to mention following several side-tracks, he eventually found a comfortable niche in 1987 as Head of Music Reference Services in the Cook Music Library at Indiana University Bloomington. He has an international reputation as a researcher of wind instruments, especially members of the flute family.

In 2011, David retired from IUB and moved to Portland, Oregon. He now practices energy healing, writes about music (now also about releasing your shackles), edits early music, edits writings for others, supports the piano-teaching studio of his wife (Lilin Chen), and actively participates in the unschooling of their 16-year-old son, Lucien Lasocki.

Although you might suspect he has no free time, in fact he loves to attend concerts, listen to Spotify in the car, eat falafel, go for walks, play tennis occasionally, watch tennis on Tennis Channel, do Qi Gong sporadically, make puns constantly, play music once in a while, read books generally about music or something to do with releasing shackles, and dance frequently. Three examples of his unsuspected life as a dancer (and not-dancer) may be found on youtube.com.

And please buy his autobiography, *I Am Alive Now: Writings from a Lifetime of Healing* (2012, 2018).

NOTES

1. "L'homme est né libre, & par-tout il est dans les fers. Tel se croit le maître des autres, qui ne laisse pas d'être plus esclave qu'eux." Jean-Jacques Rousseau, *Du contrat social; ou, Principes du droit politique* (Amsterdam, 1762), 1. I have changed what is usually translated as "man" into "human beings" with a plural verb to reflect current usage of the same concept.

2. Mark Twain, "Consistency," paper read at the Hartford Monday Evening Club, 1884. See *The Complete Essays of Mark Twain*, ed. Charles Neidler (Garden City, NY: Doubleday, 1963), 578, 583.

3. Quoted widely on the Web without a source. I've not found the quotation in the most likely source, his *Creative Evolution*, trans. Arthur Mitchell (New York: Henry Holt, 1911; reprint, Mineola, NY: Dover, 1998). I prefer not to use quotes without a source, but the ideas expressed in this quote were too helpful for our purposes for me to pass up.

4. Stephen Nachmanovitch, *Free Play: Improvisation in Life and Art* (Los Angeles: Jeremy P. Tarcher, 1990), 190.

5. Rupert Sheldrake, *The Presence of the Past: Morphic Resonance & the Memory of Nature*, rev. & expanded ed. (Rochester, VT: Park Street Press, 2012), 390.

6. "Der Aphorismus, die Sentenz, in denen ich als der Erste unter Deutschen Meister bin, sind die Formen der 'Ewigkeit'; mein Ehrgeiz ist, in zehn Sätzen zu sagen, was jeder Andre in einem Buche sagt, — was jeder Andre in einem Buche nicht sagt…" Friedrich Nietzsche, *Götzen-Dämmerung* (1889), "Streifzüge eines Unzeitgemässen," section 51. See, for example, *The Twilight of the Idols and The Anti-Christ*, trans. R. J. Hollingdale, introduction by Michael Tanner (London: Penguin Books, 1990), 115. "Die Sentenz" also means aphorism, so it seems that Nietzsche was just giving both Greek-derived and regular versions of the term with a plural verb. Accordingly, I have collapsed the sentence into the singular.

7. David Shields and Elizabeth Cooperman, *Life is Short — Art is Shorter: In Praise of Brevity* (Portland, OR: Hawthorne Books & Literary Arts, 2014), 26.

8. The *Oxford English Dictionary (OED)* has the advantage for me that we can see all the historical uses of the words, complete with quotations to set the uses in context. It has the disadvantage that many entries have not yet been fully brought up to date.

9. "So what?": reportedly a favorite saying of the jazz trumpeter and bandleader Miles Davis, immortalized in his composition of the same name, first recorded commercially on *Kind of Blue* (1959). Unlike most jazz musicians, who develop a style then keep recycling it for the rest of their lives, Davis was able to keep reinventing himself, his band, and his music for his entire life.

10. Sheldrake, *Presence of the Past*, 437.

11. If you are interested in my own experience of religion and spirituality, let me refer you to my autobiography: *I Am Alive Now: Writings from a Lifetime of Healing* (Portland, Oregon: Instant Harmony, 2012); e-book available from http://www.instantharmony.net.

12. *Oxford English Dictionary.*

13. For a useful history of schooling and its motivations, see Peter Gray, *Free to Learn: Why Unleashing the Instinct to Play Will Make Our Children Happier, More Self-Reliant, and Better Students for Life* (New York: Basic Books, 2013), chapter 3. I would also cite the courageous John Taylor Gatto, but some of his summaries that I checked didn't correspond to the sources he cited.

14. *Oxford English Dictionary.*

15. A recent meta-analysis published by the *British Medical Journal* found no association between high levels of saturated fat in the diet and heart disease. Not so for trans fats. See Russell J. de Souza, Andrew Mente, Adriana Maroleanu, Adrian I. Cozma, Vanessa Ha, Teruko Kishibe, Elizabeth Uleryk, Patrick Budylowski, Holger Schünemann, Joseph Beyene,

and Sonia S. Anand, "Intake of Saturated and Trans Unsaturated Fatty Acids and Risk of All Cause Mortality, Cardiovascular Disease, and Type 2 Diabetes: Systematic Review and Meta-Analysis of Observational Studies," *BMJ* 2015; 351; doi: http://dx.doi.org/10.1136/bmj.h3978 (published 12 August 2015). See also Malcolm Kendrick, *The Great Cholesterol Con: The Truth about What Really Causes Heart Disease and How to Avoid it* (London: John Blake, 2007).

Saturated fat was originally blamed for heart disease and other ills because of the Seven Countries Study by Ancel Keys. "The study revealed that the countries where fat consumption was the highest had the most heart disease, supporting the idea that dietary fat caused heart disease. The problem is that he intentionally left out countries where people eat a lot of fat but have little heart disease, such as Holland and Norway. Countries where fat consumption is low but the rate of heart disease is high, such as Chile. Basically, he only used data from the countries that supported his theory, a process known as cherry picking. This highly flawed observational study gained massive media attention and had a major influence on the dietary guidelines of the next few decades." Kris Gunnars, "Modern Nutritional Policy Is Based on Lies and Bad Science"; http://authoritynutrition.com/modern-nutrition-policy-lies-bad-science/; accessed 2 February 2016.

16. I believe that the first macrobiotic book I read, and certainly the most influential, was George Ohsawa, *Zen Macrobiotics: The Art of Rejuvenation and Longevity*, rev., ed. & annotated Lou Oles (Los Angeles: Ohsawa Foundation, 1965)

17. See Steven M. Druker, *Altered Genes, Twisted Truth: How the Venture to Genetically Engineer Our Food Has Subverted Science, Corrupted Government, and Systematically Deceived the Public* (Salt Lake City, UT: Clear River Press, 2015).

18. See Frank J. Jerome, *Tooth Truth: A Patient's Guide to Metal-Free Dentistry*, updated ed. (Chula Vista, CA: New Century Press, 2000).

19. See Christopher Bryson, *The Fluoride Deception* (New York: Seven Stories Press, 2004); Paul Connett, James Beck, and H. S. Micklem, *The Case Against Fluoride: How Hazardous Waste Ended up in Our Drinking Water and*

the Bad Science and Powerful Politics that Keep it There (White River Junction, VT: Chelsea Green Publishing, 2010); and Philippe Grandjean and Philip J. Landrigan, "Neurobehavioural Effects of Developmental Toxicity," *The Lancet Neurology* 3, no. 13 (2014): 330–38.

20. Adam Grant, *Originals: How Non-Conformists Move the World* (New York: Viking, 2016), chapter 7, "Rethinking Groupthink," argues that *solicited* criticism is highly beneficial.

21. See *Wikipedia*, s.v. "Shadow (Psychology)," and http://www.theqeffect.com/shadow; accessed 26 January 2016.

22. *Oxford English Dictionary.*

23. *Merriam-Webster.*

24. *Oxford English Dictionary.*

25. See Stephen Cherniske, *Caffeine Blues: Wake up to the Hidden Dangers of America's #1 Drug* (New York: Warner Books, 1998).

26. See http://www.cdc.gov/drugoverdose/data/overdose.html, http://www.cdc.gov/alcohol/index.htm, and http://www.cdc.gov/tobacco/data_statistics/index.htm; accessed 25 January 2016.

27. See John Yudkin, *Pure, White, and Deadly: How Sugar Is Killing us and What We Can Do to Stop it*, rev. ed. (New York: Penguin Books, 2013); first published as *Sweet and Dangerous* (New York: Peter H. Wyden, 1972); William Dufty, *Sugar Blues* (Radnor, PA: Chilton Book Co., 1975; New York: Warner Books, 1976); and Gary Taubes and Cristin Kearns Couzens, "Big Sugar's Sweet Little Lies — How the Industry Kept Scientists from Asking: Does Sugar Kill?" *Mother Jones*, November/December 2012; available from http://www.motherjones.com/environment/2012/10/sugar-industry-lies -campaign; accessed 26 February 2016.

28. See Mark Hyman, *The Blood Sugar Solution 10-Day Detox Diet: Activate Your Body's Natural Ability to Burn Fat and Lose Weight Fast* (New York: Little, Brown, 2014); http://drhyman.com/blog/2014/03/06/top-10-big-ideas-detox-sugar/

29. Edward O. Wilson, *Consilience: The Unity of Knowledge* (New York: Vintage Books, 1999), 58.

30. Park, *Voodoo Science*, 14.

31. See, for example, Robert Horton, "Offline: What is Medicine's 5 Sigma?" *The Lancet* 385 (11 April 2015): 1380; Rupert Sheldrake, "The Replicability Crisis in Science"; available from http://scienceselfree.tumblr.com/; accessed 8 February 2016; and John Bohannon, "Who's Afraid of Peer Review? A Spoof Paper Concocted by *Science* Reveals Little or no Scrutiny at Many Open-access Journals," *Science* 342, no. 6154 (4 October 2013): 60–65; DOI: 10.1126/science.342.6154.60.

32. Marcus T. Anthony, "Sheldrake & the Credibility Issue in Modern Science"; http://www.mind-futures.com/crisis-in-science/; accessed 8 February 2016.

33. Park, *Voodoo Science*, 211.

34. Park, *Voodoo Science*, 9–10.

35. See James L. Oschman, *Energy Medicine: The Scientific Basis*, 2nd ed. (Edinburgh & New York: Elsevier, 2016), 215.

36. The "scientific" approach to interior knowledge and its reconciliation with the scientific approach to exterior experience is the subject of Ken Wilber, *The Marriage of Sense and Soul: Integrating Science and Religion* (New York: Random House, 1998).

37. Patrick Wilson, *Second-Hand Knowledge: An Inquiry into Cognitive Authority*, Contributions in Librarianship and Information Science, 44 (Westport, CT: Greenwood Press, 1983).

38. Wilson, *Second-Hand Knowledge*, 10.

39. Wilson, *Second-Hand Knowledge*, 10, 13.

40. Wilson, *Second-Hand Knowledge*, 14.

41. Wilson, *Second-Hand Knowledge*, 25.

42. See Carrie A. Lowe and Michael B. Eisenberg, "Big6™ Skills for Information Literacy," in Karen E. Fisher, Sanda Erdelez, and Lynne (E. F.) McKechnie, ed., *Theories of Information Literacy*, ASSIST Monograph Series (Medford, NJ: Published for the American Society for Information Science and Technology by Information Today, 2005), 63–68. Their "Big6" skills are: (1) Task Definition: Define the problem; identify the information needed. (2) Information-Seeking Strategies: Determine all possible sources; select the best sources. (3) Location and Access: Locate sources; find information within sources. (4) Use of Information: Engage (e.g., read, hear, view); extract relevant information. (5) Synthesis: Organize the information from multiple sources; present information. (6) Evaluation: Judge the result (effectiveness); judge the process (efficiency).

43. For a fun exploration of some of the issues, see Leslie F. Stebbins, *Finding Reliable Information Online: Adventures of an Information Sleuth* (Lanham, MD: Rowman & Littlefield, 2015).

44. On quantum theory, I recommend Bruce Rosenblum and Fred Kuttner, *Quantum Enigma: Physics Encounters Consciousness* (Oxford & New York: Oxford University Press, 2006), which was written by quantum physicists for a lay audience and remains open to questions of consciousness in relation to physical reality.

45. Quoted in Rosenblum & Kuttner, *Quantum Enigma*, 13.

46. Rosenblum & Kuttner, *Quantum Enigma*, 150.

47. For a convenient mine of information on the Zero Point Field and its implications, see Lynne McTaggart, *The Field: The Quest for the Secret Force of the Universe* (London: HarperCollins, 2001; New York: HarperCollins,

2002; New York: Harper Perennial, 2003),

48. McTaggart, *The Field*, 20.

49. McTaggart, *The Field*, 19.

50. McTaggart, *The Field*, 23.

51. McTaggart, *The Field*, 25. For citations of Puthoff's papers, see the endnotes in McTaggart's book.

52. McTaggart, *The Field*, 26.

53. McTaggart, *The Field*, 29.

54. McTaggart, *The Field*, 29.

55. Krishna Gauci is working on a book about his ideas, *Tapestry of Being: Talks on Practical Mysticism*. With his permission, I have based the current chapter on his teleseminars, *Tapestry of Being* (May–June 2013), *The Lover's Heartbeat* (October–November 2013), and *Descent into Love* (July–September 2015), as well as discussions and email correspondence with him over the period 2011–18. Krishna is a senior teacher of Trillium Awakening (formerly known as Waking Down in Mutuality), but his Tapestry of Being teachings represent his own synthesis, based on his own experiences, his observation of the students he works with, and his continuing research on the world's spiritual traditions.

56. The title of Enza Vita, *Always Already Free: Recognizing the Natural Wakefulness that We Were Born with* (Highbury, SA, Australia: Baraka Publishing, 2015).

57. Gauci, notes to *Tapestry of Being*.

58. Sheldrake, *Presence of the Past*, 437.

59. For Sheldrake's theories summarized in this chapter, see his *Presence of the Past* and *Morphic Resonance: The Nature of Formative Causation*, 4th rev. & expanded US ed. (Rochester, VT: Park Street Press, 2009). For more

general background, see his *Science Set Free: 10 Paths to New Discovery* (New York: Deepak Chopra Books, 2012).

60. Sheldrake, *Presence of the Past*, 440.

61. Sheldrake, *Presence of the Past*, 442.

62. *Oxford English Dictionary.*

63. Sheldrake, *Presence of the Past*, 442.

64. Sheldrake, *Presence of the Past*, 441.

65. Sheldrake, *Presence of the Past*, 441.

66. *Oxford English Dictionary.*

67. Sheldrake, *Presence of the Past*, 438.

68. Sheldrake, *Presence of the Past*, 133–34.

69. See, for example, http://www.sciencedaily.com/releases/2008/12/081221220328.htm; accessed 16 January 2016.

70. Sheldrake, *The Rebirth of Nature: The Greening of Science and God* (Rochester, VT: Park Street Press, 1994), 138.

71. McTaggart, *The Field*, 47, remarks: "Sheldrake's theory is beautifully and simply worked out. Nevertheless, by his own admission, it doesn't explain the physics of how this might all be possible, or how these fields might store this information."

72. The term stems from Richard Dawkins, *The Selfish Gene* (Oxford & New York: Oxford University Press, 1976). But note that Dawkins is vehemently opposed to Sheldrake's theories about morphic fields.

73. See Richard Feynman, "Conservation of Energy"; available from http://www.feynmanlectures.caltech.edu/I_04.html; accessed 5 May 2016.

74. Robert Park, *Voodoo Science: The Road from Foolishness to Fraud* (Oxford & New York: Oxford University Press, 2000), 67, writes: "Incredible explanations invoking modern physics are sometimes offered for how alternative therapies might work, but there seems to be little interest in testing these speculations scientifically." "... there seems to be" lacks an agent, whether scientists or alternative therapists, and the author's statement is not (or no longer) true for the scientific testing, as we will see.

75. Oschman, *Energy Medicine*, 2nd ed., 251–54.

76. Oschman, *Energy Medicine*, 2nd ed., chapter 14.

77. See http://www.levity.com/alchemy/blake_ma.html; accessed 4 May 2016.

78. Oschman, *Energy Medicine*, 2nd ed., especially 251–54.

79. I don't have space to mention these discoveries here. See Oschman, *Energy Medicine*, 2nd ed.

80. *Oxford English Dictionary.*

81. Access Consciousness insists that "It's not intuition that you have; it's awareness. You define intuition as something that comes and goes, rather than awareness, which is something that is always there. Intuition is the idea that something comes to you as if by magic. But awareness is … something that is a part of who you are. As long as you define awareness as intuition, you are seeing it as something that's not instantly available to you at all times.… Every time you have an intuition, acknowledge it as awareness. Ask 'How do I expand this awareness until it's here all the time?'" Gary M. Douglas and Dain Heer, *The Ten Keys to Total Freedom* (N.p.: Access Consciousness Publishing, 2012), 88. I will incorporate more ideas from Access Consciousness into the second edition of this book.

82. Rollin McCraty, "The Intuitive Heart," in Doc Childre, Howard Martin, Deborah Rozman, and McCraty, *Heart Intelligence: Connecting with the Intuitive Guidance of the Heart* ([Cardiff, CA]: Waterfront Press, 2016), 42–48.

83. McCraty, "Intuitive Heart," 43.

84. McCraty, "Intuitive Heart," 44.

85. McCraty, "Intuitive Heart," 47–48.

86. McCraty, "Intuitive Heart," 46–47.

87. "Et remarquant que cette vérité: *je pense, donc je suis*, était si ferme et si assurée, que toutes les plus extravagantes suppositions des sceptiques n'étaient pas capables de l'ébranler, je jugeai que je pouvais la recevoir, sans scrupule, pour le premier principe de la philosophie que je cherchais." René Descartes, *Discours de la méthode* (1637); version numérique par Jean-Marie Tremblay (2002), 22–23. For a translation, see for example, *A Discourse on Method*, trans. John Veitch, Everyman's Library, 570 (London: J. M. Dent; New York: Dutton, [1912]), 26–27.

88. Deborah Rozman, "Attributes of Heart Intelligence," in *Heart Intelligence*, 30–31.

89. McCraty, "Intuitive Heart," 60, 80–88.

90. Again, I haven't found the source of this quotation in quotation books or the translations of his books that are readily available. Nevertheless, the presence of a German version on the Web ("Folge deinem Herzen, aber nimm dein Hirn mit") suggests to me that it may be genuine.

91. The title of Joe Dispenza, *Breaking the Habit of Being Yourself: How to Lose Your Mind and Create a New One* (Carlsbad, CA: Hay House, 2012).

92. I first encountered this idea in Ohsawa, *Zen Macrobiotics*, 101: "Everything changes in this relative and rotating world, monopoly and authority included."

93. Arthur Conan Doyle, *The Sign of the Four* (Philadelphia: J. B. Lippincott, 1890), 111.

94. For the American Dental Association's current statements, see http://www.ada.org/en/about-the-ada/ada-positions-policies-and-state

ments/statement-on-dental-amalgam; accessed 3 May 2016.

95. "ADA Lies Through Their Teeth About Mercury Fillings"; see https://iaomt.org/ada-lies-teeth-mercury-fillings/; accessed 3 May 2016.

96. See, for example, Randall Fitzgerald, *The Hundred-Year Lie: How Food and Medicine Are Destroying Your Health* (New York: Dutton, 2006; paperback ed. as *The Hundred-Year Lie: How to Protect Yourself from the Chemicals that Are Destroying Your Health*, New York: Plume, 2007).

97. So many books on how to release toxins exist that I hesitate to recommend any. One comprehensive book I have found useful is Nina L. Diamond, *Purify Your Body: Natural Remedies for Detoxing from 50 Everyday Situations* (New York: Crown Trade Paperbacks, 1996), not as out of date as you might think.

98. See John Diamond, *Your Body Doesn't Lie: Unlock the Power of Your Natural Energy* (New York: Warner Books, 1980). Originally published as *BK — Behavioral Kinesiology: How to Activate Your Thymus and Increase Your Life Energy* (New York: Harper & Row, 1979).

99. Anne Jensen, "The Accuracy and Precision of Kinesiology-style Manual Muscle Testing: Designing and Implementing a Series of Diagnostic Test Accuracy Studies" (D.Phil. thesis, University of Oxford, 2014). For the abstract, see http://ora.ox.ac.uk/objects/uuid:4fd95394-e812-402e-9195-6c82643eaa15; accessed 28 April 2016.

100. Machaelle Small Wright, *Flower Essences: Reordering Our Understanding and Approach to Illness and Health* (Jeffersonton, VA: Perelandra, 1988), 58–61.

101. Diamond, *Your Body Doesn't Lie*, 46–52; Diamond, *Life Energy: Using the Meridians to Unlock the Hidden Power of Your Emotions* (New York: Dodd, Mead, 1985; St. Paul, MN: Paragon House, 1995), 17–18.

102. See Lama Tantrapa's website, www.qigongcoaching.com; accessed 28 April 2016. He learned and now coaches Qi Gong within the umbrella of

Qi Dao.

103. See http://consciousdance.org/conscious-dance.php; accessed 4 February 2016.

104. See Kam Yuen, *Instant Pain Elimination: How to Stop the Pain You Feel in 2 Minutes or Less* (Canoga Park, CA: CEM Publishers, 2003); and Yuen and Marnie Greenberg, *Delete Stress and Pain on the Spot!* (Henderson, NV: Motivational Press, [2015]).

105. John Veltheim, *The BodyTalk System: The Missing Link to Optimum Health* (Sarasota, FL: PaRama, 1999); Veltheim, *BodyTalk Access: A New Path to Family and Community Health* (Sarasota, FL: International BodyTalk Association, 2008); and Veltheim, *The Science and Philosophy of BodyTalk: Healthcare Designed by Your Body* (Sarasota, FL: International BodyTalk Association, 2013). See also *Journal of Alternative Medicine Research* 3, no. 3 (2011), an issue devoted to BodyTalk and including fourteen short articles by Veltheim that demonstrate eight of the techniques..

106. Oschman, *Energy Medicine*, 2nd ed., 110. For the first scientific contribution, see Laura L. Stuve, Honghu Liu, Jie Shen, Jill Gianettoni, and Janet Galipo, "Evaluation of Body-Talk, a Novel Mind–Body Medicine, for Chronic Pain Treatment," *Journal of Pain Management* 7, no. 4 (2015): 279–90.

107. This is part of a technique I learned in a healing session with the late Gilly Adkins in 2011 or 2012. She tells me that the full technique will appear in her forthcoming book on HeartTalk.

108. Teal Swan, *Shadows before Dawn: Finding the Light of Self-love through Your Darkest Times* (Carlsbad, CA: Hay House, 2015).

109. Swan, *Shadows before Dawn*, 79–82. She actually says "What would someone who loves themselves do?", which I find singularly plural.

110. McCraty, "Intuitive Heart," 62, 82.

111. See Joe Dispenza, *Breaking the Habit* and *You Are the Placebo: Making Your Mind Matter* (Carlsbad, CA: Hay House, 2014).

112. In 2015 the founder of Waking Down in Mutuality, Saniel Bonder, chose to leave the Waking Down Teachers Association and formally registered the name *Waking Down in Mutuality* to use for his own individual work, thus prohibiting the WDTA from using it for their activities. *Trillium Awakening* was chosen as a replacement by the WDTA after consultation within the community. Although the new name doesn't convey the helpful notions of Waking, Down, and Mutuality, it does represent the threefold nature of the path.

113. See CC Leigh, *Becoming Divinely Human: A Direct Path to Embodied Awakening* (Portland, OR: Wolfsong Press, 2012), chapter 8, pp. 129–57.

114. See Marshall B. Rosenberg, *Nonviolent Communication: A Language of Life*, 3rd ed. (Encinitas, CA: PuddleDancer Press, 2015).

115. This chapter is based on Rosenberg, *Nonviolent Communication*, and Inbal and Miki Kashtan, "Key Assumptions and Intentions of NVC"; available from http://baynvc.org/key-assumptions-and-intentions-of-nvc/; accessed 26 April 2016; with additions by Sandra Amiry and Vika Miller.

116. For more information about Vika Miller's work, see her website www.thrivinglifenvc.org especially the video at www.thrivinglifenvc.org/nvc; accessed 15 March 2018.

117. My definition (Vika Miller): A belief is a thought we think over and over again, and label as "true."

118. See Laura Shocker, "This Is Your Body on Stress"; available from http://www.huffingtonpost.com/2013/03/19/body-stress-response_n_2902073.html; accessed 15 March 2018.

119. See, for example, https://www.sciencedaily.com/releases/2012/04/120402162546.htm; accessed 15 March 2018.

120. Barry Stevens, *Don't Push the River (It Flows by Itself)* ([Lafayette, CA: Real People Press, 1970]).

121. *The Complete Works of Aristotle, The Revised Oxford Translation*, ed. Jonathan Barnes, Bollingen Series LXXI/2 (Princeton: Princeton University Press, 1984), II, 1552 ("Men" changed to "Human beings" once more).

122. On the disadvantages of children hanging out primarily with their peers, see Gordon Neufeld and Gabor Maté, *Hold on to Your Kids: Why Parents Need to Matter more than Peers* (New York: Ballantine Books, 2005), and Robert Bly, *The Sibling Society* (Reading, MA: Addison-Wesley, 1996).

123. Larricchia, *Free to Learn*, 17.

124. See Gray, *Free to Learn*, chapter 5, and Dayna Martin, *Radical Unschooling: A Revolution Has Begun*, rev. ed. (Madison, NH: author, 2009). The term "unschooling" seems to have been invented by John Holt to replace Ivan Illich's "deschooling," in his *Deschooling Society* (New York: Harper & Row, 1971), although Holt came to use it interchangeably with "homeschooling." See John Holt and Pat Farenga, *Teach Your Own: The John Holt Book of Home Schooling* (Cambridge, MA: Da Capo Press, 2003), 61. For examples of how unschooling can work, see Mary Griffith, *The Unschooling Handbook: How to Use the Whole World as Your Child's Classroom* (New York: Three Rivers Press, 1998); DaNelle Wolford, "How to Learn all Subjects through Unschooling," http://www.weedemanreap.com/learn-subjects-unschooling/; accessed 26 February 2016; and Leo Babauta's blog at http://sett.com/unschoolery; accessed 9 March 2016.

125. See Julie Bogart, "Why I Gave up the Unschooling Label," http://blog.bravewriter.com/2007/10/12/un-defining-unschooling/; "Explaining Natural Learning," http://blog.bravewriter.com/2016/02/25/explaining-natural-learning-to-your-kids/; both accessed 26 February 2016; and Pam Laricchia, *Free to Learn: Five Ideas for a Joyful Unschooling Life* (Erin, Ontario, Canada: Living Joyfully Enterprises, 2012).

126. This recent sense of "deschooling" is different from the original one of Ivan Illich, *Deschooling Society*.

127. William Goldman, *Lord of the Flies* (New York: Coward–McCann, 1962), is a "Classic study of human nature which depicts the degeneration of a group of schoolboys marooned on a desert island" (WorldCat). My example caused a stir among members of the Portland Unschoolers group on Facebook, who told me that it showed I didn't understand unschooling. They made the point that anything (including video games and microwaved frozen pizza) could be a source of learning for a child, so I should trust the child's learning process implicitly. They also believed that the supportive family environment would remove any potential danger in the situation.

128. A friend who unschooled her four children, now grownup, wrote to me: "I did not keep my children home because of any educational philosophies, but because I enjoyed spending time with them and could. It is a privilege and a gift that I like to think works both ways. It was huge in my life, but, as to be expected, my children take it for granted. Being homeschooled is a fun fact, not a significant identifier in their adult lives. I am pretty sure they would have turned out just as wonderful if they had gone to school—they just had more time to explore who they were without it."

129. Gray, *Free to Learn*, 176–80. See also Pam Larrichia, "Memoir: School Failed My Son, so I Let Him Learn from Video Games," *Toronto Life*, 9 March 2016; available from http://torontolife.com/city/life/unschooling-memoir/; accessed 10 March 2016.

130. See A. S. Neill, *"Neill! Neill! Orange Peel!": An Autobiography* (New York: Hart, 1972).

131. See Gray, *Free to Learn*, chapter 5; and Peter Gray and David Chanoff, "Democratic Schooling: What Happens to Young People who Have Charge of their Own Education?" *American Journal of Education* 94, no. 2 (February 1986): 182–213.

132. Gray, *Free to Learn*, 88; *Wikipedia*, s.v. "Sudbury School"; accessed 21 February 2016.

133. See www.antiochcollege.org; accessed 20 February 2016.

134. Prescott College website, http://www.prescott.edu/explore/index.php; accessed 25 February 2016.

135. See Michael Ellsberg, *The Education of Millionaires: Everything You Won't Learn in College about How To Be Successful*, updated with a new afterword (New York: Portfolio/Penguin, 2012).

136. See especially Laricchia, *Free to Learn*, chapter "Living Together."

137. See Shefali Tsabary, *Out of Control: Why Disciplining Your Child Doesn't Work … and What Will* (Vancouver, BC, Canada: Namaste, 2013); and Grant, *Originals*, 163–67. I was tempted to call this section "unparenting," but I don't want to imply that parents are neglecting their responsibilities towards their children.

138. Tsabary, *Out of Control*, 195.

139. Adam Grant, "How to Raise a Creative Child. Step One: Back Off," *New York Times*, 30 January 2016; available from http://www.nytimes.com/2016/01/31/opinion/sunday/how-to-raise-a-creative-child-step-one-back-off.html?smprod=nytcore-ipad&smid=nytcore-ipad-share&_r=0; accessed 20 February 2016. The article is partly based on his book *Originals: How Non-Conformists Move the World* (New York: Viking, 2016).

140. Marie Kondo, *The Life-Changing Magic of Tidying Up: The Japanese Art of Decluttering and Organizing*, trans. Cathy Hirano (Berkeley, CA: Ten Speed Press, 2014).

141. Kondo, *Life-Changing Magic*, 5.

142. Kondo, *Life-Changing Magic*, 181.

143. Kondo, *Life-Changing Magic*, 182.

144. Eleanor Brownn, "The 3 Reasons Why You Are Drowning in a Sea of Clutter"; blog posted 20 November 2014; available from http://www.eleanorbrownn.com/blog; accessed 28 April 2016.

145. I highly recommend a book on this subject—one of the most beautiful books I have ever read: Nachmanovitch, *Free Play*.

146. Gray, *Free to Learn*, 143.

147. "… bless your past … that it turns to wisdom.…" Dispenza, *You Are the Placebo*, 313.